# The
# *Adventure*
## *of*
# *Philosophy*

# The
# *Adventure*
## *of*
# *Philosophy*

## Luis E. Navia

Westport, Connecticut
London

**The Library of Congress has cataloged the hardcover edition as follows:**

Navia, Luis E.
    The adventure of philosophy / Luis E. Navia.
       p.      cm.—(Contributions in philosophy, ISSN 0084–926X ; no.
71)
    Includes bibliographical references and index.
    ISBN 0–313–30976–0 (alk. paper)
    1. Philosophy Introductions.  I. Title.  II. Series.
BD21.N38   1999
100—dc21         99–14838

British Library Cataloguing in Publication Data is available.

A hardcover edition of *The Adventure of Philosophy* is available from Greenwood Press,
an imprint of Greenwood Publishing Group, Inc. (Contributions in Philosophy, Number
71; ISBN 0–313–30976–0).

Library of Congress Catalog Card Number: 99–14838
ISBN: 0–275–96547–3

First published in 1999

Praeger Publishers, 88 Post Road West, Westport, CT 06881
An imprint of Greenwood Publishing Group, Inc.
www.praeger.com

Printed in the United States of America

The paper used in this book complies with the
Permanent Paper Standard issued by the National
Information Standards Organization (Z39.48–1984).

10 9 8 7 6 5 4 3 2 1

# Contents

# *Preface*

The title of this book, *The Adventure of Philosophy*, reflects the way in which I understand the meaning of philosophy. It is an adventure that through my readings and reflections I have shared with the countless philosophers who for over twenty-five centuries have kept it alive. I also have shared it with the thousands of students who have passed through my classrooms, many among whom have felt the fascination of philosophical reflection and whose lives have been enriched by the power that flows from the ideas of great philosophers. Philosophy is above all an intellectual adventure in which we are committed to a constant search for meaning and clarity, to a relentless self-examination, and to a constant endeavor to see the world around us in a new and unprejudiced light. To do philosophy is to open wide the eye of the mind to all our experiences, to our consciousness, and to the reality that surrounds us and of which we are a part. It involves a methodic questioning of our assumptions and beliefs, a bracketing away of the 'truths' with which the social world has filled our minds, and a critical assessment of the values and convictions with which we have been brought up. It is, therefore, a liberation from the intellectual and spiritual fetters that tend to immobilize the human mind. It is an adventurous journey into an unknown continent for which there is no ready-made map and for which we possess only one tool—the use of our minds.

Unlike other studies, philosophy has no facts or hard data that we are expected to memorize and no formulas that we must mechanically repeat. It is useful to remember and identify some of the major philosophers, and the special vocabulary created by philosophers over the centuries should be understood, if for no other reason than to minimize any difficulties that may be encountered as we read philosophical texts. But aside from this, we are on our own. In philosophy, there are no self-evident principles, no unchallengeable dogmas, no body of knowledge that must be accepted. Each and every one of the statements in this book, with the exception of the few historical facts that are mentioned here and there, can and should be challenged and even contradicted if, in the light of reason, they appear to be misguided. Philosophers should neither teach nor preach, for their only task is to communicate to others their assumptions and conclusions, in the expectation that they may stimulate thoughts and responses in them. This is the spirit in which the reflections contained in this book are presented.

A comprehensive introduction to philosophy would require a text several times the size of this book and would have to include a fuller treatment of many aspects of the philosophical adventure that I discuss here only in passing. The chapters of this book, therefore, can merely give the students a taste of various issues and problems that I have found to be of interest for people who approach the study of philosophy for the first time. By consulting other books, especially anthologies that offer selections from the writings of the philosophers, the students can enrich and expand their initial acquaintance with the subject. A fruitful study of philosophy requires a very careful and patient reading of writings that are often difficult and demanding. There should always be a constant exchange of views and impressions about the writings with others, as well as a reflective and thoughtful analysis of them. Again, neither in what we read in this book nor in what we read in any other philosophy book, including the writings of the philosophers themselves, should there be anything that must be interpreted as unquestionable. Philosophy is a search, a discovery, and we are all entitled to reach our own conclusions and find our own paths, as long as we are guided by some dose of critical thinking.

In chapter 1, I wrestle with the problem of the *meaning* of philosophy and endeavor to formulate a definition—a sort of definition—of what 'doing philosophy' is. My training and my inclination force me to revert constantly to the ideas and contributions of the ancient Greek philosophers, and I make no apologies for this, even though I know that this is not, as they say nowadays, a 'politically correct' attitude. I am convinced that much of what philosophers have said and written since the time of the ancient Greeks has been an elaboration and a reworking of what the Greek philosophers said and wrote. Accordingly, in clarifying the meaning of philosophy, I appeal to the origin of the word 'philosopher' that is associated with Pythagoras, who defined himself not as a man who possessed wisdom, but as someone who was committed to the search for wisdom.

Chapters 2 and 3 are devoted to two important stages in the development of ancient philosophy, namely, the rise of philosophy among the Presocratics and the presence of Socrates. The ideas that emerged in these two stages have been of great significance in all subsequent philosophical developments. With the Presocratics, we learned for the first time to think rationally and methodically about the nature of the world, and their principles and concepts have remained, both in philosophy and in science, the basis on which we have built our understanding of the universe at large. From Socrates, especially in his search for the self, we learn valuable lessons on how philosophy should pursue its course and on how the spirit of philosophy can succeed in investing human life with a sense of purpose and meaning.

Chapters 4, 5, and 6 deal, respectively, with the issue of ethical values, the problem of the existence of God, and the question of the nature of reality. In these chapters, I have appealed to a wide range of philosophical views, both ancient and modern, and I have endeavored to shed light on a spectrum of philosophical problems, in each case showing their relevance to our own present human condition. Unless philosophy is made relevant to us, to each one of the students who studies it, it remains no more than an interesting set of historical developments, and it loses what I view as its primary value to help us make sense of ourselves and of the world in which we live, and to serve as a guide to structure the conduct of our lives. I must insist on this point. If the study of philosophy does not affect the way in which we think and live, it becomes an enfeebled and strictly academic subject of no greater value than the many subjects and disciplines that students are asked to learn and that soon after graduation they are happy to forget completely.

Two extensive glossaries are found at the end of this book. In the glossary of philosophical terms, I include definitions and brief explanations of the important theories and views discussed in the chapters. In the glossary of names, I identify all the philosophers and other significant persons mentioned in the text, in each case giving a summary of some of their contributions.

In the bibliography, I have included a selection of books and articles related to the themes and issues discussed in the chapters. Some of the cited works are by the major philosophers discussed, while others are books and articles that endeavor to clarify their ideas. Most of them are readily available in libraries and bookstores, and there are many anthologies that include selections from them. Every effort should be made to consult and read them attentively in order to give more substance to the reflections that I offer in this book.

I wish to thank my wife, Alicia Cadena Navia, and my daughters, Monica, Olga Lucia, Melissa, and Soraya Emilia, for their unfailing support in the preparation of this book. Either by reading the manuscript and commenting on it, sometimes setting me aright and forcing me to clarify my thoughts, or by showing me through the example of their lives how important philosophy is for the right conduct of life, they have made it possible for me to write a text that may prove to be useful to anyone who wishes to be initiated into the study of a subject that has engaged me already for several decades. I am grateful to Mr. Hector F. Cadena for having commented at length on many sections of this book and to Rev. Augustine Savarimuthu, S.J. for his perceptive comments on chapter 5.

# Chapter 1

# The Meaning of Philosophy

There is a story about Diogenes of Sinope, the Cynic philosopher who supported himself by begging, in which we are told that once, when asked why people are willing to give alms to the lame and the blind but not to philosophers, he said that it is because people often fear being one day lame or blind, but nobody ever expects to become a philosopher. This story, as much as the other stories about Diogenes, illustrates an important idea that can furnish us with a starting point in these reflections about philosophy. Young people dream of becoming famous and wealthy, living a long and comfortable life, learning useful and productive things that would ensure for them an important place in society, and entering the world of politics or entertainment, and have other similar aspirations. But few indeed are those who dream of becoming philosophers or of devoting themselves to the study of a subject that is as difficult and obscure as philosophy and that promises neither wealth nor success in the world. It would be a marvelous thing to come upon a child or a young person who imagines that some day he would become a philosopher, or who envisions for himself a life devoted to the study and the practice of something as esoteric, not to say useless, as philosophy, which leads us to conclude that Diogenes was perfectly correct. In his time, there were very few philosophers and there were not many people who had even a passing acquaintance with philosophy or a superficial interest in it. Among us, when the demands of education are mostly practical and vocational, philosophy attracts only a very small number of people and remains a subject generally ignored, for its immediate benefits are difficult to appreciate.

The word itself, 'philosophy', seldom stands for anything definite and can be understood in a variety of ways. Even among those who devote themselves to it and call themselves philosophers, there are divergent ideas as to what philosophy is supposed to be. The image of who a philosopher is or what a philosopher does is anything but precise. Surely, certain famous people are easily identified as philosophers—one thinks of Socrates, Plato, Aristotle, or Confucius among thinkers of ancient times and of Descartes, Spinoza, Kant, Schopenhauer, Nietzsche, Sartre and Wittgenstein among those of modern times—and universities and colleges have departments of philosophy in which courses with difficult names such as epistemology and metaphysics are taught to small numbers of students or are required as part of liberal arts courses. Libraries and bookstores usually contain collections of philosophy books that are often found next to those on religion and occult subjects. Certain common occurrences of words such as 'philosophy' and 'philosophical' can be readily adduced, as when we speak of the 'philosophy' of a political party or when we describe someone in a thoughtful mood as being 'philosophical.' In general, however, nothing more specific about philosophy or the advantage of studying it can be found. The common portrayal of a philosopher depicts someone who lives lost in strange speculations, with his head in the clouds and removed from what is useful in society, and who raises questions about issues for which society has already found adequate answers.

Nevertheless, despite this lack of understanding of philosophy and despite the uneasiness some feel when they either choose to study it or are forced to come face to face with philosophers, there is among some the suspicion that philosophy, the oldest academic discipline, is something important and essential in education, something in which we come to grips with fundamental questions about the world and about human existence, and something that remains the foundation of all intellectual endeavors. We may even be aware of the fact that the ideas and insights of great philosophers have had a decisive influence on the development of culture and human institutions. Underneath every scientific discovery and behind every psychological theory, we suspect there is a philosophical theory. All the sciences have grown out of the matrix provided by the thoughts of great philosophers, and even in the world of religious beliefs there lurk philosophical insights that have provided the rational justification for them. The development of Christianity in the Middle Ages took precisely the path that it followed because of the intellectual endeavors of philosophers such as Saint Augustine and Saint Thomas Aquinas. Revolutions, whether political or cultural, are inevitably linked with philosophical principles. The French Revolution, for instance, was ideologically shaped and impelled by the ideas of philosophers such as Locke and Voltaire, and the communist movements that so powerfully affected recent history are mostly the actualization of the philosophical world view of Marx.

Furthermore, the practice of universities of conferring doctoral degrees that include the word 'philosophy' in fields of study that are seemingly unrelated to philosophy is a testimony of the presence of philosophical ideas in all theoretical and scientific endeavors. Every Ph.D. degree—Doctor of Philosophy—whether in physics, mathematics, biology, psychology, anthropology, political science, or literature, points to the lasting presence of philosophy in the modern world. For every time we endeavor to make sense of the world, every time we raise questions about the meaning of life and the existence of the world, every time we confront ethical and moral issues, and every time we reflect on the significance of our actions, we come face to face with concepts and ideas that philosophers have examined and scrutinized for hundreds of years. Indeed, each time we become engaged in thought, we participate in one way or another in the adventure of philosophy and join hands with the countless philosophers who, since the time of the ancient Greeks, have grappled with the most fundamental issues and questions of human existence.

Still, the endeavor to define philosophy is not an easy task. The common usages of the word 'philosophy' do not reveal anything particulary clear, and neither is the way in which philosophers themselves understand the meaning of their own calling always consistent. Philosophy has been understood in so many ways that it is practically useless to attempt to come up with a definition that embraces all that philosophers have sought to accomplish. The dictionary definition of 'philosophy', moreover, is not especially revealing. It tells us that it means 'the love of wisdom' or 'the pursuit of understanding'. Terms such as 'love', 'wisdom', and 'understanding', however, have so vague a meaning that by saying that philosophy is the love of wisdom, we would not be saying very much at all. Wisdom means so many things that by defining philosophy as the love of wisdom, we fail to shed light on its true meaning. Furthermore, the ways in which wisdom has been pursued are many and depend on the culture or historical time in which philosophers have lived.

We could take another path to find the meaning of philosophy by examining how philosophers 'have done' philosophy, that is, how they have exemplified their love of wisdom or understanding, just as we might do if asked to define art by pointing to the works of artists. This path, however, apart from the fact that it would involve an unending journey, would guide us along a multitude of byways displaying a great variety. How an ancient Greek philosopher pursued his vocation and how a twentieth century philosopher 'does' philosophy may furnish us with examples of philosophical activities that do not display obviously common characteristics.

In our endeavor to arrive at an understanding of philosophy, we could examine the etymology of the word 'philosophy' and inquire into the historical origins of philosophy. When we talk about the etymology of a word, we have in mind its meaning in the language in which it was first used. In etymology, therefore, we expose to light the roots of a word and gain some understanding about its original meaning. Of course, what a word once meant and what its roots stand for in a language that is no longer spoken may be different from what it means today. Take for instance the word 'school'. Its etymology takes us back to ancient Greek, a language from which at least one third of English words are derived. The word 'school' comes from the Greek word *schole*, meaning 'leisure' or 'relaxation'. Going to school was understood among the Greeks as a time for leisure or relaxation, a time sharply contrasted with activities related to physical work. Slaves and menial workers *worked* in physical tasks and made a living through physical activity, while the leisured classes, the minority, had the privilege of spending time in leisure, or in intellectual and artistic pursuits. But who among us, especially children, would view school time as leisure time? Rare indeed is the case in which the educational atmosphere is conceived of as a time to let the mind wander at freedom or a time in which we enjoy freedom from physical labor. Thus, while 'school' and 'leisure' are etymologically related, that relationship is generally no longer valid. Nevertheless, in learning about the etymology of 'school', we go back to its roots and recapture an element that should still belong to it, because education, when it ceases to be an exciting adventure to discover the world and the meaning of our lives and becomes a practical endeavor, loses its most significant purpose and transforms itself into another kind of work, whose purpose is to prepare us to spend our lives immersed in more work.

In the instance of the word 'philosophy', the exploration of its etymology is also useful. It allows us to have a glimpse of its *true* meaning, which is what etymology itself means: the word *etymos* in Greek means 'true' or 'genuine', and the word *logos* (about which we will have much to say in subsequent chapters) means, among other things, 'meaning' or 'explanation'. Hence, etymology literally refers to the true or genuine meaning of a word. 'Philosophy' is a word derived from two Greek words: *philos* and *sophia*. The former is found in modern words such as '*phil*anthropy' (the love of people), '*phil*ately' (stamp collecting), and 'necro*philia*' (the love of dead things), and is generally translated as 'friend', in the sense in which we speak of a person or a thing being dear to us. By extension, *philos* has various other meanings related to the idea of love or affection, and the word *philia* (friendship) can be used in the sense of 'yearning' or 'desire', as when we speak of a person who has been exiled *yearning* to return to his homeland or of a sick person *desiring* to regain his health. In all instances, *philos* and *philia* convey an emotional sense that cannot be simply rendered in English by words such as 'liking' or 'interest'. Thus, a friend in the Greek sense is not someone whom we just *like* or someone in whom we have a passing *interest*, but someone whom we *love* and in whose presence we *yearn* to be.

The word *sophia* has a more complex meaning that must be clarified, for if a philosopher is conceived of as a lover or a friend of *sophia*, the meaning of this term should be understood, otherwise the object of a philosopher's yearning or desire would remain unclear. A common translation of *sophia* is 'wisdom' or 'understanding', but, as stated earlier, these terms have blurry meanings. A scientist who seeks to unravel the mysteries of the universe, for instance, can be said to be wise, and so can an eloquent and perceptive poet who verbalizes the deepest human emotions. An old person is sometimes described as possessing the wisdom that many years of experience have given him, and a religious guru, speaking in a state of hypnotic trance to enraptured followers, is at times said to be endowed with great wisdom. Even animals, when they display instinctual traits, are described as wise, and nature itself is often said to act with wisdom. In the Bible, we are reminded that "the fear of the Lord is the beginning of wisdom" (Proverbs 1:7), and God is described as the fountain of wisdom. These and similar examples of the use of words like 'wise' and 'wisdom', however, reveal meanings that are difficult to understand aside from the contexts in which they are used. They can even stand in contradiction with one another, and what is described as wise in one instance is referred to in another as being a manifestation of mindlessness, as when Saint Paul (1 Cor. 3:19) reminds us that human wisdom is foolishness in God's eyes.

In Greek, *sophia* has a history that takes us back to the time of Homer in the eighth century B.C., who used the word *sophia* in the sense of cleverness or craftiness, not as associated with what we call 'a wise guy' or 'a smart aleck', but in the sense of the wisdom necessary to envision and carry out a complex task. Homer describes a master shipbuilder as someone who possesses *sophia* about shipbuilding. Unlike the workers employed in the construction of a ship, who have the *knowledge* that is required to nail a wooden plank or tie the sail to the mast or who are proficient in some small task, the master shipbuilder has the wisdom to envision the total image of the ship and guide others to its realization. Unlike the workers, then, the shipbuilder knows how to design and build a ship, and this comprehensive knowledge entitles him to be called wise. His *sophia* or wisdom allows him to be in control of the entire operation, and to be, so to speak, on top of it at all times. This sense of 'being on top of things' is what *sophia* originally signified.

It is important to stress the difference between wisdom in the sense of *sophia* and the knowledge of details or particular tasks conveyed in Greek by the word *episteme*, the original meaning of which refers to the *acquaintance* with particular things or the bits of information that let us carry out a specific task. In modern languages, the meaning of *episteme* can be rendered by words such as 'knowledge of facts' or 'information'. It is not difficult to appreciate the contrast between *sophia* and *episteme*. We are all acquainted with people who know a great deal about a certain subject and who have memorized countless facts and dates, and yet who appear to lack the ability to make sense of what they know. The information that floats in their minds is unrelated to other aspects of experience and, like pieces of an unfinished puzzle, does not stand for anything whole or complete. Much of what takes place nowadays in education is just like that—bits of information of little value. We are often asked to memorize names, dates, facts, and statistics, but what they mean and how they are related to a holistic picture of the world are concerns that are left aside. Education becomes thereby a process of instruction and turns out to be something like a grand trivia game of no consequence. Thus, we have the impression of having at our disposal a great deal of knowledge, but what we have is mostly information that, by itself, does not amount to much. We may have much *episteme* but little or no *sophia*, for the latter refers to the ability to put together the various pieces of the puzzle that sense experience and our own ability to think provide for us. It is for this reason that *sophia* is also translated as understanding. It is one thing to know many facts, but it is something else to be able to understand what we know. We may know a poem by heart and know how many words and lines it contains and still be unable to grasp its meaning.

Factual knowledge or information, that is, *episteme*, is initially essential to gain understanding, for an ignorant person cannot be expected to make sense of anything. Had we been born blind and deaf, and unable to sense anything, our minds would probably be empty like a *tabula rasa* or a blank slate. Sense experience, that is, what we see, hear, smell, taste, and touch, furnishes us with the information that is eventually transformed into the pieces of a puzzle that through the use of reason takes shape in our minds. On occasion, however, if that information is not subjected to a process of evaluation, or, if as often happens, we are exposed to vast quantities of unorganized information and suffer from what is called 'information overflow', our minds become glutted with facts, dates, names, numbers, and others such things that, while giving us the impression of understanding, do not enhance our ability to make sense of the world. We might be walking encyclopedias and living dictionaries and yet be, at least from the point of view of wisdom, empty husks, for which reason Socrates warned his friends about the danger of too much reading and learning. Devoting ourselves to filling up our minds with information may lead to stifling our ability to think.

The issue, however, that must be clarified is what is the puzzle that the philosopher is expected to put together. The shipbuilder has wisdom about shipbuilding and has solved in his mind the puzzle of the ship. But what about the philosopher? What does he want to understand? As we reflect on how the mind of a child develops as he grows and experiences the world, we realize that from the start, but especially when the ability to speak makes itself present, there is a constant interplay between experience and thought. The child sees, hears, touches, and tastes many things each day, and retains in his memory the impressions of those experiences. Impressions and memories remain at first detached and fragmented, but at some point, when words allow him to name things, a process of integration begins to take place. It is then that his mind starts to grow and that through the use of language things are identified. For language is not merely the ability to communicate but is the means by which reality is formed in the mind. At this point, the child begins to ask questions and to inquire into the relationships among experiences. Why does fire burn? Why does the sun disappear each night? What do spiders eat, and what do they do to people? Why do certain animals fly? Where do people come from? These and other questions flow ceaselessly from every child, and as the horizons of time and space grow in his mind, they encompass more objects and aspects of the world.

At first for the child, time and space are limited to the here-now, but soon ideas such as 'later' and 'far away' appear. The world is no longer limited to his home, his family, and his surroundings but extends itself in all directions. The past and the future, understood in terms of days, weeks, months, years, and even centuries, emerge. Distances increase, and the immensity of the earth and of space is grasped. At some point beyond childhood, the world reveals itself as an endless collection of things. The child's early awareness of the processes of coming into being and ceasing to be—initially grasped in terms of birth and death—forces him to move beyond the experience of things immediately present, and discloses a reality that *was before* and a reality that *will be.* It is then that genuinely philosophical questions arise in the mind. Where does the world come from? Was there a time when there was no world? What was the world before I came into existence? What will the world be after my death? Will there be a world when I will no longer be able to experience anything? Is there a point in space beyond which there is no space? If things come into being through the agency of other things—the chicken comes from an egg that came from a hen, and people come from people—does the world at large come from something else? Things and even animals appear to have a purpose and to be organized according to some plan. Can we say the same thing about the world? Is there any grand purpose for the world as a whole and for me as a part of the world? What is the meaning of reality and what does my own existence mean in the context of the existence of the world? Is reality limited to what the senses disclose, or are there other dimensions of reality? Are the teachings of religions only illusory expectations, or do they describe something real? Ultimately, although rarely, a more complex question is raised, which looms on the horizon of every philosophical quest and which is *the* most basic question in metaphysics: Why is there something rather than nothing; that is, why does *anything* exist? If God is the creator of the world, this question also applies to God: Why does God exist?

Besides these and similar questions, others more practical and more relevant to human existence arise in young minds. Taught values by parents and teachers, there comes a point when a young person begins to raise questions about what is good and what is bad. In the presence of the diversity of moral values that characterizes most societies, and witnessing so many types of human behavior, it is not surprising that issues and perplexities related to ethics emerge in his mind. Are the values that he has been taught the only true ones? Are moral teachings just an expression of somebody's opinion? Are they relative to one's culture? Are they based on something universal and absolute? Does a moral life lead to a happy life? Why are certain customs considered acceptable while others are condemned? Aside from the unpleasant consequences of parental and societal punishments, what is the point of living according to the values of the community? Is war ever justified? Can we pass judgment on practices such as capital punishment and abortion? Does the State have the right to dictate how we should conduct ourselves? Is the government entitled to determine what is right and wrong? Are there immoral laws and, if so, on what basis can we determine this?

Every child, then, is by nature a philosopher-in-the-making, an aspiring lover of wisdom, for these and other questions and issues arise sooner or later in his mind. The process of indoctrination and the necessity of practical living, however, often succeed in relegating them to a secondary plane. Often, too, they are viewed not only as useless but as detrimental for the person and for society at large, because they tend to disorient the mind and lead to confusion and rebellious-ness. A person who questions what he has been taught is not likely to function passively in society. Furthermore, who could derive any practical benefit from thinking about such questions? How could they help us in the process of making a living and supporting a family? And is it not true that such questions, interesting as they may be, are unanswerable? What have philosophers accomplished after more than twenty-five centuries of speculation and thought? Do they not continue to ask the same questions and give answers that are at odds with one another?

There is, therefore, nothing extraordinary in the fact that society has often felt uneasy in the presence of philosophers. This uneasiness manifests itself at times as indifference and disdain, and at other times as outright hostility. Philosophers are depicted as people who live in the clouds and talk nonsense about things that nobody understands or cares to understand. For this, they have been often ignored or even removed from society. In Roman times, for instance, they were repeatedly banished or executed. Even among the Greeks, possibly the most enlightened culture of antiquity, philosophers were occasionally silenced by death, as was the case with Socrates, who was accused of talking nonsense about the sky and the earth and of corrupting the minds of the young with pestering questions and impertinent conversations. Still today, there are individuals and communities among whom even the mention of philosophy sends bad vibrations. No wonder that Diogenes insisted that there are few people who expect to become philosophers. It is important for society to maintain control over people, which is why myths and tales are invented and passed on from one generation to another, as if they were final truths. However, if the truth is already found in religious creeds, political ideologies, or scientific theories, what point is there in raising further questions? If the purpose of human life is to maintain the species through procreation and to ensure its survival through the work of every individual—like ants and bees—what advantage could there be in asking questions such as "Why is there something rather than nothing?" or "What is the basis of moral values?" Thus, young people, who initially may have sheltered in themselves a spark of curiosity, often turn out to be submissive and compliant, without the slightest desire to let their minds wander through the terrain of philosophical questioning. Immersed in diversions and pastimes, attached to traditions and to sanctioned modes of behavior, repeating mechanically slogans and phrases that mean little or nothing, and proud of the fruits of technology and science that they use and abuse without much understanding, they march passively through life. Philosophy—that is, questions and thoughts about critical issues—seldom enter their consciousness. Why should they bother with unanswerable questions and unresolvable issues from which no benefit can be derived?

Even among philosophers, we find examples of this turning away from philosophy. There was, for instance, a Greek philosopher in the fourth century B.C. named Pyrrho of Elis, who became so disenchanted with philosophy that he concluded that the only thing to say about anything, especially about philosophical issues, is nothing. Nothing can be known or explained, and nothing can be communicated through language. The only option left is to suspend judgment about all matters and to say nothing about anything. Does God exist? Nobody knows or even understands the question. And the same answer can be given to *all* other questions. His disciples, taking his ideas one step further, abandoned language and chose to remain in absolute silence. Pyrrho is traditionally viewed as the founder of skepticism, a philosophical point of view that has had followers in all ages. Closely allied to it, is agnosticism, where we maintain that truth is unattainable and that knowledge is an illusion.

Let us assume, however, that we do not want to be wholly unconcerned with philosophical questions, like Pyrrho and his followers, and that we believe that understanding is possible. We would then be in the company of some of the most perceptive minds in history, men and women from all cultures and races, and belonging to all historical epochs, who have struggled with difficult, perhaps unanswerable questions, and whose lives have been enriched by the power of ideas. For it is undeniable that removed as philosophy may appear to be from practical concerns, it can assist us in structuring our lives and attaining a clear vision of the world. Unable as philosophy may be to furnish us with final answers, it can at least provide for us, through the art of critical thinking, the tools to sort out knowledge from opinion, reality from appearance, and clarity from confusion. In this sense, then, philosophy is an adventure in the realm of ideas, an adventure from which we can learn a great deal and from which we can derive the mental discipline that is essential for a good and meaningful life.

As we have seen, the word 'philosophy' means 'the love of wisdom'. Ancient biographers tell us that this word was coined by Pythagoras, a Greek philosopher of the sixth century B.C. Little is known with certainty about his life, and no writings can be attributed to him. Like Buddha, Thales of Miletus, and Socrates, Pythagoras communicated his teachings only orally. Thus, for information about his life, we must rely on what others wrote about him. Although it is difficult to determine the truth about the origin of the word 'philosophy', we can assume that Pythagoras had something to do with it. At any rate, we do not encounter this word before his time. He was born around the year 550 B.C. in Samos, an island in the Aegean Sea. As a young man, he was already proficient in geometry and other sciences, and in time his knowledge became enhanced by travels to places like Egypt, Persia, and perhaps India. Later in his life, he settled in Croton, a Greek town in southern Italy, where he lived many years and where he died. He developed a great reputation as a wise man, a sophist, for it was believed that he had mastered various fields of study: geometry, astronomy, geography, music, and others. He held certain ideas about the world that earned for him an important place among his contemporaries and that would ensure for him a lasting influence in later times. He taught, for instance, that number is the essence of all things and that the world is explainable in terms of mathematical theorems, because all things are manifestations of numerical relations. Underneath the world perceived through the senses, he believed, there is an underlying reality that permeates and structures all things. This reality, which he identified with number, can be grasped by the mind and can be explained by means of rational analysis. Even sounds are expressions of mathematical arrangements. The Pythagorean theorem, which states that the square of the hypothenuse is equal to the sum of the squares of the sides of a right triangle ($a^2 = b^2 + c^2$) and which was a major discovery in mathematics, owes its first formulation to him.

According to Pythagoras, the earth is a sphere at the center of the universe, around which the sun, the moon, and the stars move in circular orbits. He understood all things and events in the universe as expressions of harmonious relationships, and even human existence, he insisted, obeys universal harmonic rules. In Croton, he founded a school, where many philosophers, both men and women, studied all sorts of fields, especially those related to mathematics. There, under his guidance, they reflected on the puzzle of the world and endeavored to make sense of its pieces. The Pythagorean community, as Pythagoras' school became known, is the prototype of the universities and colleges that would later on emerge in the Western world and that have maintained alive the love of wisdom that animated its founder.

Pythagoras' reputation for wisdom grew with each passing day. His word, at least among his disciples, was like the expression of the truth, and his ideas about the world and the human soul were accepted as dogmas. There was a saying in antiquity in which we hear that the universe contains three kinds of intelligent beings. Foremost, of course, is God (or the gods) and last, are human beings, but between them—well, there is Pythagoras. After his death, a report about his origin circulated throughout the Greek world. A man as wise as Pythagoras, could he be the son of an ordinary man? Could his father have been just a human being? No, Pythagoras had to be the son of God, and so the story was passed along that his mother had become pregnant through the intervention of Apollo, the god of wisdom. This story would also be told in later times about Plato. It is understandable that great wisdom and uncommon intelligence are explained by ordinary people only in terms of some miraculous divine intervention. Yet, Pythagoras did not see himself as anything more than a human being. Had he heard the story about his origin, he probably would have dismissed it as a pious fiction. His reputed *possession* of wisdom was a fact only for those who surrounded him. How could he possess wisdom, if only God, he said, can be wise? Not in mortal creatures like human beings, but only in God, can we expect to find *sophia*, that is, true understanding. We can imagine that they would say to him, "Pythagoras, but can you not be wise, knowing so much and having unraveled the mysteries of the world? You have traveled to distant lands and have gathered information about so many things. You have mastered the art of measuring things and have explained the movements of the stars. You have taught us the rules that govern music and the human body and have enlightened us about how societies should be organized. You know about the soul and about its fate and wanderings after death. You have attained in your life more than anyone else. If you are not a sophist, that is, a man of wisdom, what then can you be?"

In his answer to this question, we come upon the first occurrence of the word 'philosophy': "I am," we can imagine him replying, "only a *philosopher*, that is, a man who does not understand most things and for whom the world is always a source of wonder. Like others, I was born only yesterday and shall die tomorrow, and my time on the earth is but a moment of no consequence. Much of my life has been spent in meaningless distractions and in sleep, and in sustaining my body. My senses are imperfect and limited, and I only see and hear those things that are near me, and always from *my own* subjective perspective. I cannot see the world through anybody else's eyes. My memory, like that of others, is short and defective, and when old age will come, it will be even shorter and more defective. How can anyone say, then, that I am wise? How could I have attained that which only God possesses? I am only a curious man who lives in wonder and who is moved by a desire to make sense of things. Like a child lost in a vast wonderland, I inspect all things that come my way and take note of the events and phenomena that I witness, always in a state of amazement and always reflecting on my experiences. I have come to certain conclusions about the world that I have passed on to you, in the hope that you can do to them what I have done to my own thoughts and experiences, that is, question and refine them and perhaps set them aside as unimportant or misguided. After my death, others will come with other teachings, other 'truths', that will contradict and invalidate those to which I have been attached. Other visions and theories about the world will be expounded and defended, and foolish are those who will announce them as the truth. For the truth is not a human possession, a commodity, that can be found and kept. It is rather a process and a search, an adventure of the mind, a moving towards the receding horizon of human experience. This horizon, however, has no limits, for which reason the truth cannot be pinned down, captured, found, or announced as an infallible dogma or as an article of faith. You can call me, if you wish, a philosopher, not a sophist, for that is only what I am. I am a man moved by a *philos*, a yearning, for *sophia*. A mortal man—and that is only what I am—cannot hope to be anything more than that. The expectation of finding wisdom in this world is an illusion."

We can learn a great deal from this statement. It reveals the sense of wonder that, as Aristotle reminds us, lies at the source of the philosophical impulse. In his description of himself as a child lost in a vast wonderland full of surprises and amazing phenomena, Pythagoras captures well the essence of philosophy. He contrasts the immensity of that wonderland with his own insignificance. What is a human being in the context of the universe? What is our own planet, our solar system, or even our galaxy? Contemporary astronomy discloses frontiers that would have left Pythagoras and all other ancient philosophers in a state of bafflement. We are now accustomed to measure space in light years. In these terms, the distance between the earth and the moon is slightly more than one second, and that between the earth and the sun, about eight minutes. Yet, galaxies have been identified at distances of over ten billion light years. Thus, the point that we occupy in space—we, who once were proud to be that for which God created the heavens—is negligible: in space, we amount to practically nothing. Our sun is only one among billions of stars in our galaxy, which is only one among billions of galaxies in the known universe. Other aspects and regions of the universe may exist, and other dimensions of reality may even coexist with the reality with which we are acquainted.

Likewise in the context of time, neither we as individuals nor our nations and cultures nor even our species are of any consequence. We measure our lives in decades and the history of our nations in centuries. The history of our civilization can be traced back several thousand years, and the origins of humanity several million years. Yet, the earth and the solar system have been in existence for several billion years, and still other components of the universe have existed for a longer time. What, then, is *one* human being or even *one* culture in so vast a universe? If we convert the history of the earth since its formation into one year, several facts emerge. If we assume that the earth was formed on January 1, we would have to wait until September to find the first forms of life. The emergence of primates would have to wait until December 30, and the first human-like creatures until noon of the last day. The pyramids of Egypt would be built forty seconds before the end of the year, and Christ would die twenty seconds after the building of the pyramids. Those historical events to which we attach so much importance, the French and the American revolutions, would flicker for a moment a few seconds before midnight of December 31, and then we, too, would disappear into the abyss of the past, devoured by the passage of time, only to be replaced by other beings about whom we do not have even the slightest idea. How, then, can anyone claim to have solved the puzzle of the universe?

In the course of human history, theories and views about the universe emerge and engage the imagination of many, only to be subsumed under new ideas and explanations, or to be discarded as erroneous. As information increases and as technology furnishes us with ways to extend our senses and store the memories of our perceptions, the puzzle of reality appears more and more complicated and mysterious. Still, moved by a sense of curiosity and guided by the need to make sense of the world, we persist in advancing ideas and theories. This is what philosophy means, that is, the urge to answer questions and invent explanations, always, however, aware of our inadequacy and limitations and never, if we are to remain true to the spirit of philosophy, convinced of the absolute truth of what we think and say about the world.

Still, there are some who see themselves, their culture, or their nation as the center of all things, and who claim to have attained a clear understanding of the universe and of the meaning and purpose of human existence. One finds them everywhere and at all times, sometimes preaching from the pulpit and acting as the mouthpieces of God or teaching dogmatically the 'truths' revealed by science or instilling among the masses political ideologies that are supposed to contain the truth. Even among philosophers, it is not rare to find some who insist that *their* ideas, *their* insights, and *their* conclusions disclose the truth. In all of them, there is a certain blindness that incapacitates them to see beyond themselves and an arrogance that convinces them of the privileged nature of their point of view. These are the traits that Pythagoras, in refusing to call himself a sophist, rejected. Reality, he knew, is not only more complex than we imagine, but perhaps more complex than we can imagine and, therefore, it is foolish to claim for oneself the knowledge and the wisdom that are not attainable by human beings.

We can learn from Pythagoras an important lesson that can be gathered from the study of philosophy. This lesson teaches us never to take for granted the truth of what is taught, what is found in books and newspapers, what preachers and politicians proclaim, what the media disseminates, what public opinion enthrones as the standard, and what society declares to be the truth. We must, therefore, be willing to subject to analysis and scrutiny everything that comes our way, every idea, every religious belief, every political slogan, every fact and figure, and even our own thoughts and convictions. We must be ready to experience the world anew, as a child experiences the novelty of his world, and be prepared to raise questions until we are satisfied that what we hear from others and what we ourselves discover is reasonably and tentatively acceptable. To develop a consistently skeptical attitude about all things and to examine all things under the light of critical thinking—that is what philosophy teaches. If we are unwilling or unable to let reason inspect our ideas and beliefs and those of others, either because we are intellectually lazy or because we prefer the comfort and security provided by accepted 'truths' and norms, then philosophy is not an undertaking in which we should participate. We might even be able to define philosophical terms correctly and know about what philosophers have said and written, but unless we are committed to independence of judgment and critical thinking, we will not have come even close to what Pythagoras meant when he called himself a lover of wisdom.

We should distinguish Pythagoras' coining of the word 'philosophy' from philosophy itself. No one *before* Pythagoras' time spoke of himself as a 'philosopher', for this word did not exist. Nevertheless, philosophy, as the search for understanding, did not begin with him. Long before him, not only in Greece but in other places, and even before the beginning of written history, people like Pythagoras must have existed, although on rare occasions, for the clarity of mind and the courage to confront fundamental questions are not often found. Frequently, the natural philosophical impulse to wonder about the world and to understand its mystery is drowned under the weight of societal pressures. Yet, philosophers emerge from time to time. Among the ancient Greeks, for instance, the earliest known philosopher was Thales, who lived in the sixth century B.C. and about whom we will have much to say in the following chapter. With him, then, the history of philosophy in the Western world begins, not because he was the first person to devote himself to philosophy, but because *we* do not have reliable information about other philosophers before his time. Only in this limited sense, then, can we speak of him as the first philosopher.

The arrival of Thales coincides with a critical moment in the history of civilization, when writing began to be widely used to record events and to express ideas. This moment has been called the alphabetical revolution. It introduced writing as a form of communication, side by side with the spoken word, and allowed for information to be stored and passed on from one generation to another. A quantum leap in sophistication was bound to take place and, in fact, it did, especially among the Greeks, whom we credit with the oldest known philosophical and literary writings. Anaximander, an associate of Thales, is said to have written the first book. After him, books appeared everywhere in the form of scrolls generally made of papyrus. Two centuries later, huge libraries were filled with volumes upon volumes in which the work of philosophers was recorded and studied. This revolutionary trend that began among the Greeks would then pave the way for the development of ideas, of which we, twenty-five hundred years later, are the heirs.

The history of philosophy extends thus from the sixth century B.C. to our own time. It includes innumerable philosophers who represent all cultures and races, and it encompasses every imaginable approach to *the* problem of philosophy—the meaning of reality at large and the meaning of human existence. It contains, too, all sorts of solutions and answers, so it would be useless to look for a common denominator, except for the commitment to examine the world from the point of view of reason. Philosophers have seldom been at ease in the presence of dogmas or rigid beliefs, for such things stifle the mind and thwart the imagination. Confronting fundamental questions, the philosophers' stance has been not to accept what has been taught simply because it has been taught, but to review the evidence and arrive at conclusions supported by reason.

We divide the history of philosophy into three periods, namely, ancient philosophy, medieval philosophy, and modern philosophy. The first begins with Thales in the early sixth century B.C. and ends sometime around the fifth century A.D. at the end of classical times. Thus, between Thales and the last ancient philosopher, one thousand years elapsed. Most of the philosophers of this period were either Greek or Roman, although philosophers can be found in other cultures, among whom we could mention Confucius, a Chinese philosopher of the sixth century B.C. The first stage of ancient philosophy was characterized by an interest in cosmology, that is, by an attempt to develop rational theories about the structure and nature of the universe. Paramount among the endeavors of these early philosophers was the discovery of universal principles and concepts for the explanation of nature. In this stage, philosophy and science were indistinguishable. Interesting ideas were advanced about the elements of nature, the shape of the earth, and the structure of the universe, and about other issues, some of them related to metaphysics and epistemology. The early philosophers are known as the Presocratics, because they lived before Socrates or were his older contemporaries. In general, their philosophical orientation was *objective* in the sense that their major preoccupation was with questions and issues about the world at large, not with matters specifically related to human existence.

Three among the most important philosophers in history belong to ancient philosophy: Socrates, Plato, and Aristotle. In them, we come upon magnificent examples of how the philosophical impulse that moves people to ask questions can be guided through the use of reason to create complex and challenging philosophical views. In them, we are in the presence of what can be considered to be the highest development of the human mind, for even when we find that their answers are inadequate, or when their theories have been set aside by later philosophy or by science, they still force us to come to grips with fundamental issues that cannot be ignored.

During Socrates' time, that is, the second half of the fifth century B.C., philosophy became increasingly preoccupied with concerns related to human existence, and ethics was a subject to which philosophers devoted considerable attention. This can be seen, for instance, in the philosophies of Plato and Aristotle. In later years, when the culture of the ancient Greeks became the common culture of what is known as the Hellenistic world, various influential schools of thought arose in which ethical and political preoccupations dominated the foreground. Thus, in Cynicism (a movement that grew out of the ideas and style of life of Diogenes) and in Epicureanism (a school of philosophy founded by Epicurus) the key problem was how to reach a condition of happiness and how to live a good and moral life. In Stoicism, an important school of philosophy that is traceable to Socrates, ethical considerations were also of critical value. These and other philosophical currents were exceedingly influential throughout the Hellenistic world. Eventually, as the presence of religious currents from the Near East grew and spread among the Greeks and the Romans, philosophy became blended with religious ideologies and ways of life such as Christianity and Judaism, which in their turn prepared the way for the arrival of medieval philosophy.

In medieval times, from the end of the Roman Empire to the beginning of the Renaissance, religious faith, supported by the power of the Church, held the upper hand in most human affairs. This was the age of faith. Philosophy, which is often a reflection of the prevailing culture, became dominated by the need to rationalize religious beliefs. Thus, for almost one thousand years, medieval philosophers, beginning with Saint Augustine and culminating with Saint Thomas Aquinas, pursued philosophy under the guidance of religious beliefs. Their major concern was to bridge the gap that separates, on the one hand, an explanation of the world based on faith and, on the other, a rational account of reality. This was the case not only among the Christians but also among the Jews and the Moslems. The examples of Maimonides and Averroes illustrate the ways in which philosophy became subservient to religious beliefs. Thus, for instance, medieval philosophers did not generally raise genuine questions about the existence of God or about the purpose of human life but became involved in accounting rationally for beliefs based on faith. The ethical questions that had preoccupied the Greek philosophers were answered in accord with what religion taught about human life. The ultimate purpose of every human being, medieval philosophers remind us, is to serve God, obey his commandments, and thereby gain eternal bliss. The independence of mind that had characterized the Greek philosophers, and their willingness to subject ideas to critical appraisal, were replaced by an acceptance of faith, which stood as the initial step and the final destination in all philosophical inquiries. First, we must believe and then we can endeavor to make sense of our faith in the light of reason. Saint Anselm of Canterbury put it succinctly: philosophy must be understood as "faith seeking understanding." This intellectual climate tended to create unfavorable conditions for the development of new ideas about the world, for if truth is already found in sacred scriptures and in the teachings of the Church, what could be the point in exploring other possibilities about the nature of reality and about moral values? How could independent judgment and critical thinking be possible under these circumstances? The mind of the medieval philosopher remained generally bound to faith and to unquestionable assumptions that prevented an open-ended search for understanding.

Philosophy, when independent of dogmas and unchallengeable beliefs, may take us to unexpected destinations and to unpredicted conclusions, for it is guided only by reason. On the horizon of every genuine philosophical investigation, the world reveals itself as a grand mystery, a vast and unknown reality, and the mind, as Aristotle observed in his *Metaphysics*, can be compared with someone who is in chains and yearns to secure his freedom, that is, his release from ignorance and perplexity. In a philosophy that is subservient to religion, however, precisely because of its commitment to faith and to a set of beliefs, the mind is *bound*—the very word 'religion' is etymologically derived from a Latin word that conveys the sense of being *bound* or *tied*. This is why much of medieval philosophy often gave rise to disputations about words and phrases and to controversies about the interpretation of religious and philosophical texts without advancing significantly our understanding of what experience and thought reveal about the world. To some extent, then, the world of medieval philosophers remained enclosed within the barriers created by religious faith. Still, despite these limitations, much can be learned from the study of medieval philosophy. It exemplifies a series of intellectual adventures, in which perceptive and revealing insights about the world and about human existence were achieved. Faith can provide an alternative avenue along which the puzzle of reality may be put together, and what some of the medieval philosophers sought to accomplish was to demonstrate that *that* avenue does not have to run contrary to the path outlined by reason. In seeking to understand their faith, they remained committed to a life devoted to the search for wisdom.

It is impossible to maintain human curiosity indefinitely bound by restrictions. Sooner or later, the mind liberates itself from the limitations created by religious creeds, by political ideologies, or by the modes of thinking with which society seeks to control people. Thus, at the end of medieval times, major changes began to occur as the need for intellectual freedom was felt throughout Europe. The monolithic structure of the Church was challenged and eventually broken, and important discoveries in science and the geographical expansion of the medieval world paved the way for a new beginning, the Renaissance, a period of cultural rebirth, during which an effort was made to return to the climate of classical times. Beginning in the fifteenth century, then, the independence of judgement that had characterized Greek philosophy was resurrected among philosophers, and reason was declared once more the court of judgment in human affairs. The discovery of numerous lost Greek manuscripts and their publication in the newly invented printing press were critical in bringing back to life the ideas and insights of the Greeks, not only in philosophy but also in the sciences, especially astronomy and mathematics, as well as in the arts. Greek authors were carefully studied both in their original language and in translations that made their works accessible.

The recovery of classical philosophy from oblivion signaled the beginning of a period in the history of philosophy known as modern philosophy. In it, once more we witness, especially in its initial stages, the same critical and questioning mood of the Greeks. In the sixteenth and seventeenth centuries, for instance, philosophers such as Bacon, Descartes, Spinoza, and Locke, among many others, insisted that philosophy must be understood as a rational exploration of the world, in which we should not be forced to begin with preconceived assumptions or with unquestionable premises. Philosophers felt compelled to disregard the conclusions and the methods of their medieval predecessors and attempted to begin their exploration of the world from scratch, so to speak, as if whatever earlier philosophers had accomplished was of no great value. In doing so, they gave expression to a most important lesson in philosophy, about which we spoke earlier: let us take nothing for granted and let us not be willing to accept blindly what others have said about the world. At the beginning of every philosophical investigation, then, literally everything should be called into question, and the philosopher, not unlike a child who experiences the world for the first time, must raise question after question, without being satisfied until in his own mind things are reasonably clear.

This spirit of independence has characterized the course of philosophy until our own time and has been decisive in the growth of the natural and human sciences. The world, once again, has become a spatial and temporal immensity that needs to be explored. Rational analysis and a critical examination of the methods employed in our pursuit of understanding, including the language in which we raise and answer philosophical questions—these are some of the most important tools that modern philosophy has made available. Through their use, many philosophical views have been developed during the last five centuries, and through them, too, the natural and human sciences have grown.

During the first stages of the development of philosophy among the Greeks, philosophy and science were inseparable. The philosopher was then someone who endeavored to understand the world at large, both its physical aspects and those that transcend the realm of what is physical. The scarcity of information about the world made it possible for ancient philosophers to become versed in what in later centuries would become the sciences and to attain an encyclopedic knowledge. Aristotle, for example, wrote on fields such as physics, astronomy, biology, zoology, psychology, and politics, as well as on subjects that have remained the domain of philosophy such as metaphysics, epistemology, and ethics. Given what was known then about the world, it was possible for a philosopher to embrace all that was known. Information—*episteme*, that is, facts and data—was exceedingly limited. Little was known about the earth and the universe, and simple sense perception was the only means of exploration. Neither telescopes nor microscopes, for instance, had been invented. Hence, what was known was insignificant in comparison with what has been made accessible to science through technological means. It is, nevertheless, remarkable that despite such limitations, ancient philosophers succeeded in making so many insightful comments about the world.

Beginning with the Renaissance, knowledge in the sense of information has been growing at an enormous pace, and what we are witnessing today is an explosion of information. There is more to know with each passing day, and the facts and data that are available are limitless. It has become, therefore, necessary for the sciences to break away from their original philosophical source. It is no longer possible, as it may have been in ancient times, to have a comprehensive knowledge of the world, because the world has literally grown immensely around us, and the frontiers of knowledge have been extended in all directions. Since the Renaissance, then, the natural sciences, whose aim is to gain an understanding of the physical world, and later on the social sciences, whose object is to shed light on the complexities of human existence, have been following their own paths and have remained attached to an empirical approach: observation is for the scientist the point of departure in all his endeavors. And because of the increase of knowledge, the sciences have become more specialized, so that what one scientist observes and analyzes is often seemingly unrelated to the concerns of other scientists. Thus, the world gives the impression of being a mosaic of varied colors and shapes in which there is no unity and no underlying common denominator.

One of the major tasks of philosophy during the last few centuries has been to serve as the intellectual common ground for the specialized and disparate wanderings of the sciences. The philosopher raises questions about the meaning and adequacy of scientific methodology, about the cohesiveness of scientific theories, about the meaningfulness of scientific language, and about the value of science in the context of human existence. The scientist talks about some discrete aspect of the world—the stars, the evolution of the species, the human body, or human emotions—but the philosopher reminds us that the world is, after all, one, a *uni*verse, governed by universal laws, for the understanding of which certain general principles must be grasped. He insists that there are fundamental questions and issues that remain on the horizon of human knowledge and that cannot be ignored. These questions and issues are today the essence of the philosophical adventure in which we participate whenever we endeavor to understand the world.

Living as we do in the midst of an explosion of information and possessing the technology to acquire more and more knowledge, we may be under the impression that the puzzle of the world is becoming clear and that its pieces are now falling neatly into place. Yet, on reflection it appears that the words of Pythagoras quoted earlier have even more relevance now than in his own time: wisdom, that is, true understanding, is not a human possession, but is only a human aspiration. The fundamental questions raised by ancient philosophers remain, despite all our accomplishments, basically unanswered, and our predicament is, as Kant noted, that such questions are *both* unanswerable *and* unavoidable. The following chapters of this book will illustrate this apparently unfortunate human circumstance. We say apparently unfortunate, because in reality it is far from that. Perhaps the most wonderful thing about being human and being endowed with a clear mind is the ability to confront the mystery of the world and to be able to raise questions about the meaning of reality. In Plato's account of Socrates' trial, we learn that when the jury sentenced him to death, Socrates remarked that he welcomed death because it might give him the opportunity to travel to another world, where he would continue doing what he did while in this world, that is, asking questions. There, he would question famous people and renowned Sophists about their pretended wisdom. He ironically observes that there, since he will be already dead, they could not sentence him to die. His questioning would then be unending.

# *The Discovery of the Mind*

The oldest historical records of philosophical activity in the Western world take us back to the early sixth century B.C., that is, more than twenty-five centuries ago, specifically to Miletus, a Greek city on what is today the southwestern coast of Turkey. Then and there, a group of philosophers known as the Milesian Rationalists appeared as the first representatives of a long line of thinkers who have kept alive the search for understanding that goes by the name of philosophy. Unquestionably, as noted in the previous chapter, philosophy must have been present in human communities long before their time, because, as a natural tendency of the mind to raise questions about the world, philosophy is found whenever and wherever human beings live. Even among primitive peoples, we can assume, some spark of philosophical thought can be detected. In the history of civilization and in the life of the human species, twenty-five hundred years are not a long time. Thousands of years before the sixth century B.C., ideas must have been conceived by human beings, and even complex philosophical views might have been developed. Compared with other ancient cultures, that of the Greeks is relatively new. They themselves, as attested to by historians such as Herodotus and philosophers such as Plato, recognized the fact that they were newcomers in comparison with the Egyptians and the Indians, and had they been acquainted with the Chinese, they also would have granted to them a claim to greater antiquity. When the pyramids of Egypt were built, two thousand years before the time of the Greek philosophers, nothing is known about the presence of ideas among the inhabitants of what would later become Greece. Yet, the Egyptians possessed the scientific knowledge necessary to construct the pyramids and possibly even a sophisticated understanding of the world.

Still, the problem is that historical knowledge about the *intellectual* achievements of cultures that preceded that of the Greeks is lacking. There are impressive yet silent monuments and inscriptions on stone and sketchy papyrus writings, but much more cannot be secured. The accomplishments of cultures more ancient than that of the Greeks cannot be denied, but the intellectual processes that made them possible remain shrouded in a cloud of mystery because of the absence of written records. For this reason, when we attempt to reconstruct the history of ideas, we are forced to begin with the Greeks. With them, records in the form of books began to appear, which allows us to draw a line of conceptual development among them. The alphabetical revolution made it possible for them to translate into writing what had previously been confined to oral traditions. Events and accomplishments became permanently recorded, the passage of years and seasons was calculated and codified, distances were estimated and sometimes measured with precision, geographical maps were drawn with surprising accuracy, and, most important, ideas and views about the world were written down and disseminated. In a sense, then, human experience, instead of being a mere collection of unorganized perceptions and impressions, was arranged and ordered on the basis of concepts and principles. For the first time, the idea of progress—a moving ahead in a set direction—became a reality, especially in what concerns the human aspiration to make sense of the world.

It is *not* that the Greeks *invented* philosophy or that, by introducing an element of order into human experience, they *discovered* the mind. We could not say that any given culture *invented* music or art, for those are ingrained components of all human life. Likewise in the case of philosophy: long before the Greeks, there must have been philosophical ideas in other cultures, although rarely and among few individuals, for philosophy is not a common occurrence in *any* culture. All that we mean, therefore, when we speak of Greece as the birthplace of philosophy is that among the Greeks, we come upon the oldest historical records that give testimony of a systematic philosophical and scientific activity that can be documented by an appeal to written records. It is for this reason, then, that we must begin with them.

We have the names of many among the earliest philosophers. We also know a great deal about their cultural background and have some information about their ideas and views. Unfortunately, however, hardly anything remains of what they wrote, and some of them, moreover, are believed not to have written anything. Thus, our information about them is confined either to scant fragments from their writings or to what others wrote about them sometimes centuries later. Still, a reasonably clear picture of the earliest stage in the history of philosophy can be reconstructed, a picture that allows us to appreciate not only the greatness and vigor of their intelligence and the agility of their imagination but also the extent to which their views were decisive in the shaping of ideas in later times. There is no exaggeration in saying that what philosophy and science have accomplished since their time has been to a great extent a reworking and an expansion of the concepts and principles that they created.

The earliest philosophers are known as the Presocratics, because they belong to a time *before* Socrates (469-399 B.C.). The oldest among them was Thales, who was born around the year 620 B.C. Thus, between his birth and the mature life of Socrates, two hundred years elapsed, a period characterized by an extraordinary degree of intellectual activity among the Greeks. If in our own age we are experiencing an explosion of information, in that of the Presocratics what took place was an explosion of ideas, not only in philosophy but also in other intellectual endeavors such as history and poetry. Somehow, then, culture moved on to a higher plateau of sophistication, and the first known manifestations of critical and mature thought emerged. The human world rose from a condition of unorganized and random experiences, and the mind assumed a controlling role in the quest for understanding.

Many Presocratic philosophers can be identified by name, most of whom became engaged in writing down their ideas. At the outset of this revolutionary period, philosophy developed in cities and communities that were distant from Athens, which was then the center of Greek life, and from other mainland cities. We find the philosophers mostly in regions of the eastern Greek world, specifically in the cities that Greek colonists had established on the coast of what was known as Asia Minor. It is in these frontier places that philosophy first appeared among the Greeks, as was the case of Miletus, where the three first philosophers were born—Thales, Anaximander, and Anaximenes. Founded by Athenian settlers sometime around the year 1100 B.C., Miletus grew eventually into a major city. By the sixth century B.C., it had become a metropolis, second in size only to Athens. Its cosmopolitan population included not only a large number of Greeks but also Persians, Egyptians, Jews, and other ethnic groups. There are reports that in its streets and marketplace all sorts of languages were spoken at all times and that in its temples all kinds of religious rituals took place.

This atmosphere of cultural diversity, together with the affluence of the population, created a climate of tolerance that allowed people to pursue their interests undisturbed and in freedom. The oldest manifestations of what may be called a democratic form of government belong not to the Athenians, as is often maintained, but to the Milesians, who learned early in their history that cities and countries are best governed when many people participate in the processes of framing the laws and carrying on the functions of government. The concept of freedom of speech—expressed in Greek by the word *parrhesia*, which literally means 'the ability and willingness to say it all'—is one among the many character- istics of the Milesian culture. Unlike other Greek cities of that time and unlike practically all non-Greek cities, Miletus was free from the political and social restrictions that prevent people from expressing their ideas. It was not by a mere coincidence that when the Greeks of Asia Minor were conquered by the Persians at the end of the sixth century B.C., Miletus was the city that led the revolt against them.

Undoubtedly, Miletus' cultural and political characteristics must have contributed to the rise of philosophy in its midst. If we combine these characteristics with the intelligence of its Greek population and with the richness and flexibility of ancient Greek, we should not be surprised to encounter among the Milesians impressive intellectual accomplishments. Cultural diversity allows people to confront ideas and points of view that, precisely because they are different and varied, often compel them to examine their own and to develop a critical and searching attitude. Those who live in a closed cultural environment seldom grow intellectually beyond the confines of their own culture. Affluence, moreover, gives people the opportunity to free themselves from the necessity to work for a living and can furnish them with the required leisure to let the mind wander through the world of ideas. Leisure, as Aristotle observed, is a necessary condition for the development of the mind, and when joined with intellectual abilities, it can provide a fertile ground on which thought can flourish. When, however, as often happens, leisure is not accompanied by a keen mind, it generally leads to a life of boredom and wastefulness. In the case of the Milesians, however, this latter circumstance was not the case.

If to the cultural diversity and affluence of the Milesians we add the political and social freedom that characterized their city, then we have some of the necessary ingredients for the birth of philosophy among them. Had the early philosophers lived elsewhere, especially in authoritarian or religiously restrictive communities, or in a society caught in webs of unquestionable traditions, their revolutionary and ground-breaking observations about the world would not have been tolerated. In the Bible (Leviticus 24:16) we learn that he who blasphemes against God or who even questions his existence must be stoned to death. How could have a culture that accepted and practiced this biblical injunction endured for long the presence of philosophers who raised questions about the world and who reached conclusions that were at variance with those of ordinary people or with the teachings of the authorities? How could have any other city tolerated their dismissal of what most people accepted as the truth? The freedom enjoyed by the Milesians ensured that the philosophers among them would at least be left alone to express their ideas.

Thales is often referred to as the father of philosophy, a designation that only means we have no reliable information about other philosophers before his time. Hardly anything can be affirmed about his life, aside from the fact that he was born in Miletus around the year 620 B.C. His death, some eighty years later, is said to have occurred when he fell into a ditch while observing the night sky: he was so lost in thoughts about the universe that he failed to see what was immediately in front of him! His unwillingness to write down his ideas forces us to rely on what others wrote about him. There are reports that he came from an affluent family and that he was a successful businessman. Early in his life, it seems, he traveled extensively—Egypt, Persia, India, and other places are mentioned. We are also told that he knew a great deal about the movements and positions of the stars and that he was an expert navigator who used his knowledge of the stars in his journeys. From his acquaintance with the Egyptians, he learned the elements of geometry—a rudimentary kind of trigonometry—that allowed him to estimate distances by measuring angles. Through his expertise in engineering, he is credited with having diverted the course of a river, the Meander, that used to flow through Miletus. He also played some role in the political affairs of his city, acting as advisor to the government and undertaking various diplomatic missions.

The oldest scientific model of the universe is associated with him. He envisioned the earth as a rectangle-like plank floating on water and covered by a dome, below which the sun, the moon, and the stars moved from east to west. Water, too, he thought, surrounded the dome. Obviously, this cosmological model has little in common with those of modern times and does not resemble even those of his immediate successors. Nevertheless, it stands as the *first* scientific, that is, rational, conception of the universe, one that would be challenged and refined by those who came after him and that would start the course of evolution through which science has moved since his time. Neither in philosophy nor in science should we expect to find truth and completeness in any one stage of development. Neither should we judge ideas and theories by a final standard of truth and accuracy, but only as steps in an ongoing intellectual journey toward a more adequate understanding of reality. One day our own cosmological views will appear to our successors as simple-minded as those of Thales appear to us.

An important accomplishment of Thales was his prediction of a total solar eclipse that was visible in Miletus in the year 585 B.C. Unlike lunar eclipses, which are relatively easy to predict even with minimal astronomical information, solar eclipses, because of their rarity and limited area of visibility, are difficult to foresee. A successful prediction of a solar eclipse, at a time when correct astronomical information was scarce and when such an event was the cause of consternation, must have been an impressive feat, and so was the case with Thales' prediction. It happened just as he had forecast it, which brought him great fame. We do not know how he managed to make his prediction, especially in view of his primitive idea of the universe. The sun, the moon, and the stars, according to him, rise daily in the east out of the water that surrounds the earth and are plunged in the west once more into the water. How, given such a view, a successful prediction of a solar eclipse could be made is not easy to figure out. We suspect that his acquaintance with Babylonian tables of eclipses made his prediction possible. For his prediction of the eclipse and other accomplishments, Thales earned a tremendous reputation for wisdom and was called a sophist, that is, a man of wisdom. There is a story that the Delphic oracle, about which we will have much to say in chapter 3, declared Thales to be the wisest man in the world, for who could have known as much as he did? Who could have reached a more impressive understanding of the world? But if he had been acquainted with the term that several decades later Pythagoras would use to describe himself—a 'philosopher', that is, someone who yearns to attain wisdom but who does not possess it—Thales might have described himself in the same way. A great mind seldom falls into the temptation of arrogance, and we can take it as a general rule that whenever we come upon an arrogant or conceited person, whether in ideas or in any other respect, we are in the presence of a small mind, and *this* was certainly what Thales was *not*.

Aside from his prediction of a solar eclipse, something else can be affirmed about Thales. He maintained that everything in the world is water and only water. If his description of the universe is the first recorded cosmological model, then his contention that everything is water is the oldest documented philosophical *and* scientific statement. Still, what a strange statement! What could its meaning be, and why would have Thales come to so bizarre a conclusion? Does it not run contrary to what every sensible person, now and during his time, knows about the world? We know what water is—we drink it, bathe in it, float on it, observe how it flows in rivers, see it fall from the clouds—and we know that stones and earth, fire and air, and other things are *not* water. But now the man who has been called the father of philosophy comes along to tell us that *all* things are nothing but water and that aside from water there is nothing else. No wonder the story about his death mentioned earlier, which describes him falling into a ditch while looking at the stars and immersed in thought, because one would have to be blind or nearly blind not to realize that fire, earth, air, and other things are simply not water! Imagine how a thirsty child would react if, when asking for water, we would offer him a brick, saying to him that according to Thales everything is water, including a brick.

Yet, the issue may not be so simple. It is true that through sense perception we learn to recognize and identify things by their characteristics. The senses teach us that a glass of water and a brick are two very different things, and for this, even the intelligence of a baboon is adequate. The world appears to us to be made of a variety of things, composed of different elements and substances that are endowed with specific characteristics that distinguish them from one another. It enters into our awareness as a collection of independent things that come into being and pass out of existence. Birth and death are circumstances that appear to be inherent in all things, including ourselves, and every mature person can imagine a time when he did not exist and a time when he will no longer be. Experience, however, is related only to the present moment and the immediate place and does not disclose by itself the relationships that, through the use of imagination and the ability to retain sensations in memory, are recognized in thought. We see at any given time only a few things and hear a few sounds. What we see and hear is always determined by the limits of our senses, and these reveal only a small part of the world that surrounds us. It took a great deal of effort, for instance, to figure out that the phases of the moon are the result of the changing angles at which solar light is reflected on the lunar surface, a discovery that is attributed to Anaxagoras, a Presocratic philosopher who lived one hundred years after Thales. The senses alone would never have allowed us to reach this conclusion, and the same can be said about all knowledge that is beyond our immediate field of experience.

We said in chapter 1 that the first lesson that can be learned from philosophy is not to take anything for granted, even if everybody around us vouches for its truth and merit, and even if it has been accepted for hundreds of years. We must subject our perceptions, ideas, and beliefs to constant critical examination and be prepared to abandon them, even if by so doing we choose a path contrary to that of the multitude. To make this point as clear as possible, Diogenes would walk backwards among the Athenians or would go to the theatrical performances only when people were already leaving. Now we can refine a bit more this lesson in the context of Thales' insistence that all things are water. What philosophy teaches us is that what we see, hear, touch, smell, and taste reflects only the surface of the world. Beneath our impressions, there is a reality that transcends what the senses reveal, and in order to recognize this reality, we must move beyond simple sense experience. This is what ideally distinguishes a child from a thoughtful person. We say ideally, because the passage from childhood to maturity is not always ensured by the passing of time. Age does not ensure that a mature mind has developed, and there is some truth in a comment of Heraclitus, a Presocratic philosopher, who tells us that most people live in their waking hours as if they were asleep and are guided only by the appearances of things, as if they were children. The impressions of the senses are for most people their only dimension of reality, for which reason it is easy to dupe them and make them believe all sorts of childish things.

The success of senseless political ideologies and fantastic religious myths, as well as the grip with which in our own time the media controls the masses, are easily explained by reference to people's inability to move beyond impressions and sensations. This inability is especially evident when great crowds congregate around some belief, some creed, some point of view. Amid slogans and cliches, and stupefied by shouting and chanting, the crowds are always willing and ready to accept whatever is presented to them, and enthrone public opinion as the source of truth in politics, religion, and morality, and especially in what passes for reality. For them, illusion and fact, fantasy and reality, are indistinguishable. For this reason, Socrates advised his friends to disregard always the opinions of the many, for they neither contain any truth nor promote the search for understanding. There was an important Athenian general and statesman named Phocion in the fourth century B.C. who was at some time a student of Plato and who took Socrates' advise quite seriously, making it a practice to vote in the Athenian assembly always against the wishes and proposals of the majority. He thought that by so doing he had a better chance to choose the right way, for, according to him, if most people believe that something is true or good, it is probably false or bad. Not surprisingly, after a long and turbulent political life, he was executed by the Athenians in the same fashion as Socrates was—by hemlock poisoning.

Neither is it surprising that every major step taken to advance knowledge has involved a struggle against prevailing points of view. Whether in philosophy, in science, in art, or even in religion, change comes only after what is held to be the truth is challenged, as exemplified by Thales' ideas. Living at a time when myth and superstition were the only tools that allowed people to make sense of their experiences, he took on the task of creating a new way of looking at the world and launched an onslaught against the beliefs of his contemporaries, creating thereby a conceptual revolution that would shape the course of human thought in subsequent ages. Instead of the ordinary and traditional ways of understanding the world, which were based on unorganized experiences or on beliefs sanctioned by traditions, he proposed a new approach. Reason, not sense experience or blind belief, was the new approach, and for this purpose he and the philosophers who came after him developed several concepts that have remained the basis of philosophy and science.

We still need to clarify, however, the meaning of Thales' statement that all things are water. This statement runs contrary to what we know or rather seem to know about the world, because things other than water do not appear to be water. Yet, what Thales taught is that beneath the differences that distinguish one thing from another, there is a universal element into which all things are eventually resolved and from which they originate, and this element, according to him, is water. Thus, we are in the presence of an attempt to explain things in terms of *one* element, for which reason we speak of his philosophy as an example of monism, a term derived from the Greek word *monos*, which means 'one' in the sense of 'only one'. With Thales, therefore, things arise from water, return to water, and, what is more important, *are* water, which is the one and only reality as the universal element that undergoes changes and transformations and as the underlying basis of all things. The fact that ordinary sense experience does not show us that this is the truth is inconsequential. The senses, as Heraclitus insisted, are generally bad witnesses in judging what is true. If we guide ourselves by what we see, hear, and touch, we are inevitably led into a mistaken and limited view of reality.

What could have led Thales to conclude that all things are water is a much debated question that has been answered in various ways, although all such answers are guesses. Let us remember that he probably wrote nothing. It has been argued, for instance, that the fact that water is essential for all forms of life might have influenced him. Also, living by the sea and being a navigator could have contributed to his idea. Likewise, he must have realized that water has the peculiarity of presenting itself to us in three forms—as a solid when frozen, as a liquid in its 'normal' state, and as a gas when transformed into vapor. Three distinct forms and yet the same thing. This might have led him to the conclusion that water is the basic element, although this is also only a conjecture.

More significant, however, is the idea that things are explainable in terms of *one* element. The word used in Greek to refer to what we call 'element' is *arche*, a word that has several interrelated meanings. It can mean, for instance, 'beginning', in the sense in which something begins in time or is the basis of something else. It can also refer to the idea of something that is ancient or primitive. Still another meaning suggests something that is in control or in command, or something that governs other things. Thus, in modern languages we have words like '*archaic*' (old or ancient), '*archae*ology' (literally, the study of ancient things), '*archi*tecture' (understood as the technique of dealing with the structure and the foundations of buildings), '*arche*type' (an original pattern of which things of the same type are copies), '*arch*bishop' (a higher bishop), '*arch*angel (an angel who rules over other angels), and so on. In its philosophical sense, which applies to Thales' conception of water (although we do not know if he used the actual word *arche*), it conveys the idea of an underlying element that undergoes changes while remaining the same.

This element, then, when frozen *appears* in the form of ice, when compressed in the form of rocks and earth, when heated or rarefied in the form of vapor or air or even fire, and at other times in the form of what we ordinarily identify as water. In most of its manifestations, it does not seem to be water, but, in fact, it is water and only water, for aside from water, there is nothing else. As *the* universal and material element of the world, it neither comes into being nor ceases to exist. Things, as temporary and changing manifestations of water, come and go, emerge in time from other things, and disappear into other forms. They have a beginning and an end and are forever undergoing processes and changes and are formed and deformed, created and destroyed. Water, however, remains unaltered and undiminished, and is not subject to changes, except in its manifestations. Thus, we cannot speak of water as having come into existence, for it is eternal and always the same and cannot be conceived of as having been created by something else. If the universe was created by God or gods, these, too, must be still another, more ancient form of water and as physical and material as the universe. Needless to say, this is a startling beginning for philosophy and science. It opened a new chapter in the history of human thought, and it discloses a view of reality that is radically different from what sense perception teaches us and from what ordinary people, both during Thales' own time and in later times, must have thought about things. It reveals an uncommon level of intellectual sophistication made possible by the presence of a powerful and adventurous mind that was willing to set aside what the senses conveyed about the world.

The question whether in saying that all things are water Thales was right or wrong is not an appropriate question, for in philosophy *and* in science we should not look for absolute truth, but only for a movement toward the truth. His theory about the nature of reality was just that—a theory, that is, a vision of what things are, which is what the Greek word *theoria* conveys, namely, the view of the landscape that we have as we climb a mountain. As we climb higher, our view becomes greater and fuller, and earlier views are replaced by others that encompass more details and a wider horizon. The search for truth is similar. With each passing stage in the history of ideas, our view gains in scope and breadth, but since our ascent has no limit, this view will never be complete. Twenty-three centuries after Thales, Lavoisier, a French chemist and the father of modern chemistry, discovered a gas that he named 'hydrogen', which literally means 'made from water'. In the periodic table of elements, hydrogen occupies the first place, because its chemical weight is the lightest in nature. In recent times, science has concluded that more than ninety percent of the known universe appears to be made of pure hydrogen and that *all* the elements are atomic transformations of hydrogen that take place in the stars and especially in the stellar explosions in which old stars die and new stars are born. If Thales were to come back to life, he might say that his vision of the universe was not entirely mistaken. Today we still tend to hold a monistic view of the universe, for things, at least those that are material, are believed to be transformations of *one* element, namely, hydrogen. Water, moreover, which is two-thirds hydrogen ($H_2O$), is the compound that he identified as the universal element. Still, the issue of how close he came to express a scientific view that resembles those of modern times is only a historical curiosity.

More important is the fact that he began the search for understanding along a path drawn by concepts such as *arche* and universal principles such as the conviction that only through rational analysis we can expect to make sense of the world. It is for this reason that we are justified in speaking of him as the father of philosophy and science, and as the man who discovered the mind. He could have chosen something other than water as the primordial element and could have said that all things are air, fire, mud, or anything else, and his importance in the history of ideas would have remained undiminished. His search for *one* unifying concept was sufficient to ensure for him the place that he occupies. His immediate successors, Anaximander and Anaximenes, also Milesian philosophers, rejected his idea of water as the primordial *arche*, but remained attached to monism. They still sought to resolve all things into one universal element.

Anaximander, to whom we owe, among other things, the oldest book, as well as the belief that the species are transformations of earlier extinct ones and the view that the universe contains an infinity of suns and earths, displaced water from its privileged position and insisted that there was something even more basic. He called this element the Infinite or the Indefinite (expressed in Greek by the word *apeiron*), for it was, he thought, so removed from sense perception that no distinguishing characteristics could be assigned to it. Nothing definite, then, could be said about it, and no known object could be identified with it, for which reason he spoke of it as the Indefinite, although as material as water. It is also worth noting that Anaximander corrected Thales' model of the universe. According to Thales, the flat earth floats on water and is surrounded by a dome. For Anaximander, neither the water that supports the earth nor the celestial dome is required. The earth, still a flat rectangle, lies at the center of *our* world, suspended in space and supported by nothing, while the sun, the moon, the planets, and the stars move *around* it. Beyond our world, there are other worlds, in which other suns and stars move around other earths. In his view, the universe is infinite and has no boundaries either in time or in space. In those other worlds, other living creatures, like and unlike those on earth, also exist. Before our world was formed, other worlds existed, and when our world will disintegrate, other worlds will arise out of its remains in an eternal cycle of transformations.

Anaximenes, an associate of Anaximander, set aside the idea of the Indefinite as the primordial *arche* and put in its place something more readily identifiable, namely, air. Things are transformations of air, brought about by processes such as condensation and rarefaction. With him, we are still in the presence of monism (all things are one) and materialism (all things are made of a material element), but the specific ideas of his predecessors stand rejected or corrected, which is what we should expect as we advance from one philosopher to another. Just as Anaximander moved beyond Thales and developed a new vision of the world, so did Anaximenes with respect to Anaximander. And after them, the same occurred with later philosophers. Pythagoras, for instance, dismissed the idea of a rectangle-like flat earth and introduced, possibly for the first time, the geocentric idea of a spherical earth that sits motionlessly at the center of the universe, an idea that would be dominant until the sixteenth century when Copernicus proposed a heliocentric model in which the sun was placed at the center.

More significantly, Pythagoras abandoned the monism of the Milesian philosophers and introduced the notion that all things are explainable in terms of *two* elements, namely, mind or soul, and matter, which is an example of what is known as dualism. His introduction of the mind or soul as one of the basic components of reality allowed philosophy to move beyond the materialism of the earlier philosophers. For them, all things are reducible to a material element or *arche*, and anything that is not composed of matter does not exist. The human soul, conceived of as an immaterial entity that is different from the body and that can exist apart from it, would have had no place in the world of the Milesian philosophers. Likewise, the belief in an immaterial and transcendent God would have been foreign to them. With Pythagoras, however, a door was opened to a more comprehensive and complex understanding of reality. Moreover, his conviction that the transformations undergone by things are expressions of mathematical relationships, and that all processes, whether physical or spiritual, are controlled by numerical laws, paved the way for a thoroughly rational approach to the world, which eventually made it possible for science to use mathematics as the primary tool to explain the world.

After Pythagoras, philosophical activity moved along various paths, always following the guidelines set by the Milesian philosophers. Among the Presocratics who came after Pythagoras, we come upon Heraclitus, who conceived of the world as an ongoing transformation of a primordial element that he identified with fire. Like a flame, which feeds itself from the surrounding air and gives off part of itself in a continuous exchange of matter, things are always in a state of flux, constantly changing, while remaining only *apparently* the same for a short time. The world, he said, is like a river whose waters are always running and passing and are never the same. Only the substance of things, that is, fire, remains unchanged, for which reason the permanence that sense experience reveals about them is only an illusion. In the eternal cycle of birth and rebirth out of fire, worlds upon worlds come into being and are destroyed, just as things emerge from other things and are the sources from which others arise. Fire alone remains unchanged amid all the transformations.

We also come upon examples of pluralism, a view that conceives of the world in terms of *several* elements. Empedocles, a philosopher from Sicily, spoke of earth, water, air, and fire as the basic components of material things and of the soul as the essence of spiritual reality. The Milesians' monistic interpretations of the world were inadequate for him. Every material thing, every physical object, according to him, contains a part of each one of the four primordial elements, and it is only the proportions in which they are found in things and their arrangements in them that create their distinctions. A brick, a bone, a flame, and an insect, all contain earth, water, air, and fire but in specific arrangements and proportions. This idea of Empedocles had a profound influence on later thinkers, including Aristotle, and both in antiquity and in medieval times it served as the basis on which philosophers tried to account for the physical world.

Other Presocratics extended pluralism even further. Anaxagoras, to whom we owe scientific contributions such as the correct explanation of the phases of the moon and an estimate of the size of the sun (an estimate that, although mistaken, is the earliest attempt to measure a celestial body), maintained that the elements are neither one nor many but infinite in quantity and variety. If space and time have no limits, neither do the elements. He spoke of them as 'seeds' and envisioned them as eternal, uncreated, and unchangeable. Things are combinations of 'seeds', and the preponderance of certain kinds of 'seeds' in them is what distinguishes one thing from another. From this point of view, then, the universe is an infinite and eternal collection of elements or 'seeds' that cannot be numbered or classified, because there is no limit either to their number or to their shapes or forms. Everything, according to Anaxagoras, contains the 'seeds' found in every other thing. Even the smallest thing is a microcosm that reflects the macrocosm and is a whole universe onto itself. A piece of meat, for example, contains 'seeds' that once were in water, fire, air, rocks, human flesh, leaves, and, in fact, in everything else. What we call meat, therefore, is only a collection of all sorts of 'seeds', in which the most numerous are those of meat, which allows us to identify the object as a piece of meat. For Anaxagoras, however, the combinations of the primordial 'seeds' are guided and controlled by certain universal laws that ensure that the kinds of things that constitute the world remain reasonably constant and that the world does not turn out to be a random place in which things could come from anything. His world remains, therefore, rational and explainable despite the infinity of the 'seeds'. This point is important, because it reflects a critical principle of Presocratic philosophy, which teaches us that whatever happens in the world, and whatever changes take place in it, are conditions that come about as a result of a law of nature. The world is not a random and unexplainable collection of things and happenings but a rational and organized structure that can be known and understood only through the use of the mind.

Another important Presocratic philosopher who advocated pluralism was Democritus, a contemporary of Socrates. In him, we come upon an example of an encyclopedic man of extraordinary knowledge and erudition. He wrote on all sorts of subjects, including astronomy, physics, mathematics, biology, botany, ethics, and politics. From his works, however, only fragments remain, but from these, as well as from the secondary sources, we can form a clear picture of the man and his philosophy. According to him, reality can be understood in terms of atoms. All things are composed of exceedingly small bits of matter that are indivisible and unbreakable, which is what the Greek word *atoma* signifies. He conceived of the atoms as eternal, for, unlike things that come into being and pass out of existence, they were never created and cannot be destroyed—they simply *are* eternally and cannot cease to be: once an atom, always an atom. They are, moreover, infinite in the sense of having no limit in number. Like the universe, which has no limits in space, they are limitless. Things come into being as passing and unstable collections of atoms, and their destruction happens when their atoms move on to integrate other things. Birth and death are, therefore, only apparent, for the constituents of things remain forever unchanged in the cycles of transformations that we call the world. Eternally moving throughout infinite space, the atoms are the only things that we can call reality, for nothing else exists aside from them. The human body is itself composed of atoms, and its growth and stability are made possible by a constant influx and excretion of atoms. As a person, then, I am nothing but an aggregate of atoms that have existed in other things and that, after my death, will remain in existence in other things. Even consciousness is either only physical atoms or the effects of the movements of atoms within me. I am nothing but a temporary and fragile collection of material particles that is destined to become extinct amid the endless cyclical changes of the universe.

In the atomistic materialism of Democritus, we come to the end of the first stage of philosophy among the Greeks. What began two centuries earlier with Thales' statement that all things are *one* universal element comes now to a close with Democritus' affirmation that the atoms are the only reality. A review of the process by which philosophy first arose among the Greeks and its progress among the Presocratics discloses the presence of certain concepts that underlay their views of the world. Among such concepts, *four* can be identified. The first one is *arche*. It conveys, as we have seen, ideas such as beginning or origin, but its philosophical sense among the Milesian Rationalists is that of the basic material, the stuff, out of which things are made. In the case of a marble statue of Napoleon, for instance, its *arche* is the marble of which it is made, and its form is that of the French emperor. The same marble could have been carved to create the statue of someone else, and then we would have a different statue but the same *arche*. What is significant about the concept of *arche* is that it reveals the Presocratics' conception of reality. Unlike most people of their time and other times, they suspected that beneath the appearances of things—their colors, shapes, and other distinguishing characteristics—and beneath their individuality, there is a permeating unity, a basic common denominator that, through reflection and thought, can be identified with one or several primordial elements that undergo changes while remaining always the same. Whether we choose water, air, fire, atoms, or anything else makes no difference. What matters is the realization that the real world *is not* what it *appears to be.* Reality and appearance are *not* the same.

Another significant aspect of the concept of *arche* is related to the idea that change affects only the transformations of the primordial element or elements.

Hence, it is necessary to view the world as timeless or eternal. Time happens to things, but not to the world, which explains why the world, understood, of course, not as the earth or even as the known physical universe but reality at large, has no age. Stars, planets, and all other things have an age and exist in time, but not the world. It is senseless to ask questions about the beginning of the world or about its creation. God as creator becomes an unnecessary assumption to explain the existence of the world, and the myths through which people attempt to make sense of the world turn out to be just that—poetical tales with no basis in reality. For this reason we are justified in regarding Thales and others among the Presocratics as thinkers who stood in opposition not only against simple sense experience as the source of truth, but also against all mythological modes of explanation.

The second concept, *physis*, is somewhat more complex. From the term *physis*, we derive words such as 'physics' and 'physical', although these words do not always reflect the ancient meaning. Among the Greeks, *physis* conveyed the idea of something that emerges, remains for a while, and then disappears. The phases of the moon can serve as an example. We can see how in the course of fifteen days the shapes of the moon undergo a repetitious cycle, beginning with a new moon and progressing until, fifteen days later, we have a full moon. During the next fifteen days, it grows thinner, until it disappears once more, only to begin a new cycle. Countless other examples come to mind. The growth of hair on a man's face is also a *physis*. At a certain age, hair begins to appear on the face and reappears with predictable regularity after each shave. It does not happen normally to women. Why only to men and after a certain age? Why not in childhood and why only on the face? It would be surprising to find a full beard on the face of a newborn child, because that would run contrary to what we are accustomed to expect. We learn to anticipate certain predictable sequences, and these sequences are what the Greeks called *physis*. We see and experience it everywhere—in the movements of the sun and the stars, in the regularity of the tides, in the recurrence of the seasons, in the growth of animals and plants, in the behavior of chemicals, and, indeed, everywhere. Unexpected happenings cause surprise and even fright, not because they are in themselves unpredictable or random, but because we lack enough information about the processes of nature that they manifest. Things behave inflexibly in accordance with their *nature*, that is, their *physis*. Thus, the world reveals itself as a collection of processes, as an all-encompassing *physis*, and it is the regularity and the predictability of such processes that sustains the philosophical and scientific dream of reaching a greater understanding of the world. This is what the Presocratics, beginning with Thales, firmly grasped. The mind takes the information provided by the senses and arranges it in patterns and sequences and discovers the underlying order of nature that permeates all things.

*Physis* is generally translated as 'nature', but this word is as vague as the word 'physical'. When we speak of nature, images of the jungle, the undergrowth, the forest, wild animals, and natives in remote lands come to mind, and when we refer to something as physical, we envision something that is tangible. In both cases, however, our understanding of 'nature' and 'physical' does not capture the sense of *physis*. In *this* sense, things are physical or natural, not because they can be perceived, but because they exhibit changes and transformations that are part of a regular process. Whatever exists in time is physical and natural, for which reason theologians insist that God is not physical, not because he may be beyond our senses, but because he does not exist in time and is not subject to change. He lies outside or beyond nature, for nature is the regularity exhibited in the processes of physical things. When we say, for instance, that it is the *nature* of water to boil at a certain temperature or that the *nature* of light is to move at a certain speed, we give expression to what the Greeks meant when they spoke of *physis*.

We can now move on to the third concept of Presocratic philosophy, *logos*, a word that has several meanings, the most common being 'word' or 'statement'. It also means 'account' or 'explanation', and, more generally, 'reason'. Events in nature happen as a result of some sufficient and necessary reason, and both the reasons why things happen and our explanations of those reasons are expressed by the word *logos*. Furthermore, our capacity to recognize and verbalize those reasons, that is, our ability to think *and* speak, is also *logos*. The realization that the world, which may give the impression of being random and whimsical, is a *logically* arranged collection of processes presupposes the presence of a mind (*logos*) that is capable of recognizing order and structure, as well as a language (*logos*) through which these can be expressed. The logic (*logos*) of the world corresponds to the logic (*logos*) of the mind.

The world can, therefore, be called a *kosmos*, which is the fourth concept of Presocratic philosophy. The word *kosmos* originally conveyed the idea of beauty or arrangement, as in the modern word 'cosmetics'. A well-designed building, a well-trained horse, and a disciplined army were described by the adjective *kosmos*. Beginning with the Presocratics, however, this word was also used as a noun to refer to the universe, just as we do when we call it the cosmos. In their eyes, the universe exhibited the highest degree of beauty, arrangement, and order. Instead of being conceived of as a collection of random occurrences and accidental happenings, the universe reveals itself as an ordered structure. The processes of nature (*physis*) and the transformations of the primordial element or elements (*arche*) are all controlled by certain universal laws (*logos*), which is precisely what renders the world a *kosmos*.

Here, then, the four major concepts of Presocratic thought converge to reveal the oldest vision of reality in the history of philosophy. As the four cornerstones of that vision, these concepts allowed the Presocratics to invest their experiences with a sense of order. Whatever the world might be, one fact remained unquestionable for them: it is rational and, therefore, knowable and explainable, and the method or way to advance toward the goal of solving its mystery is the use of the mind. It is for this that we can attribute to them the discovery of the mind. They insisted that understanding cannot rely exclusively on simple sense perception or cannot be based on fantasy and myth or cannot be derived from emotional states of consciousness, for in these approaches what is revealed is at most the appearance of things, not their reality. Their introduction of rationality as the primary tool of knowledge and understanding made it possible for philosophy and science to arise among them, and there is no exaggeration in saying that whatever philosophical ideas and scientific views may have emerged during the twenty-five centuries after them, all of them have been efforts to reformulate and rephrase their questions, refine and correct their answers, and, in a word, rehearse their attempts to come to grips rationally with fundamental problems and issues.

An important characteristic of Presocratic philosophy is its cosmological orientation. In general, the Presocratic philosophers remained engaged in questions about the world at large, about its elements and components, and about its structure and processes. Among them, the world was the primary *object* of their philosophical search, while the *subject*, that is, the mind that searches for understanding, remained mostly in the background. Their orientation was, therefore, *objective*. During the late fifth century B.C., however, a change took place, and a *subjective* orientation emerged. Human existence, with all its complexity and its problems, rose to the surface as a critical aspect of the philosophical adventure, and philosophers began to raise questions related to ethics and the purpose of human life. Epistemology, which deals with the nature, sources, and limits of human knowledge, also became a source of interest. The self—who and what I am, not only as a person, but also in the context of the existence of other selves—gained in significance as a subject of philosophical reflection. More important than questions about the nature of the world were the issues concerning how I ought to live my life and the meaning of my existence as a human being. We will examine in the following chapter this reorientation and will follow the path taken by philosophy under the guidance of Socrates. We will see how the concepts and principles created and used by the Presocratics remained generally intact, although their application, instead of being directed at the world at large, became relevant in the attempt to understand human existence.

_____ *Chapter 3* _____

# *Socrates and the*
# *Pursuit of the Self*

With the arrival of Socrates we enter into a new stage in the development of philosophy, as if we had been compelled to make a fresh beginning. The cosmological explorations of the Presocratics, their search for the elements of nature, and their efforts to make sense of the universe at large now give way for a new direction and a new approach. For Socrates, it is no longer the world that needs to be understood nor the laws that govern the processes of nature nor the structure of the universe nor the constitution of matter nor the nature of time and space. For him, there is another concern of greater urgency, one that eclipses every other concern with which philosophy could be preoccupied. With him, then, philosophy turns its attention in another direction. He insisted that instead of looking outwards, that is, toward the world, we should turn our glance inwards, that is, to the being that we are, each one of us in his own individuality. The world, with all its elements and stars, steps aside to let the self, the human soul, occupy the only place of prominence worthy of consideration in the adventure of philosophy. More important than questions concerning the elements of nature or the processes responsible for the emergence of things or metaphysical inquiries that pretend to clarify the essence of Being are those that have to do with the self or the soul and those that are relevant to the conditions that lead to happiness and to a virtuous life. It is not the world but the human condition that engages Socrates' imagination. His approach, especially as manifested in the method which is associated with him —the Socratic method—would have a profound effect on the way in which subsequent philosophers have pursued their calling.

As a historical figure, Socrates is a paradox. On the one hand, a great deal has been written about him. His ideas have been the subject of scrutiny on the part of many people including philosophers, historians, and psychologists, and his name is mentioned in all sorts of contexts, almost as if he were an indispensable presence in any intellectual endeavor. Yet, on the other hand, hardly anything can be affirmed about his life or about his ideas, especially in view of the fact that no writings can be attributed to him. Concerning his life, only a few details are well established. He was born in Athens in 469 B.C. His father was a sculptor or rather a stonecutter, and his mother was a midwife. He lived in Athens all his life, and only on rare occasions is he known to have visited other cities. Perhaps twice he served in the Athenian army, distinguishing himself for bravery and endurance. When he was a middle-aged man, he was portrayed in a comedy by Aristophanes, a playwright, as a demented man with a great ability to dupe and confuse those who came to him for counsel. In this comedy, entitled *The Clouds*, Socrates appears as a man whose views were dangerous for society and who should not be tolerated.

Nothing is known about his education. Whatever he learned seems to have been the result of his own efforts, for no teachers are associated with him. He became a notable figure in Athens and had friends and acquaintances among the oligarchs and also powerful enemies who succeeded at last in undoing him. Many aspiring youths became attached to him and tried to emulate his way of life. Among the most important were Xenophon, an Athenian general and historian, and Plato. He was married to a woman named Xanthippe and was the father of three children. Living a life of austerity, simplicity, and poverty (for he was not inclined to work for a living), he spent his time conversing with people in the marketplace and in the streets, asking questions and discussing issues about all sorts of things, especially about moral and political matters. His questioning earned him the reputation of being a busybody, a pest, comparable to a gadfly, which is an insect that stings cattle and awakens them from slumber. He insisted that he could not teach anybody, because he had neither knowledge nor wisdom to impart. He maintained that the only thing he knew was that he knew nothing or hardly anything and that he was always in a state of perplexity about most things. The fact that he knew that he knew nothing, he would add, made him the wisest man in the world, for the recognition of his own ignorance made him truly wise. He would often say that people who claimed to know a great deal about all sorts of things were more ignorant than he, because whereas he knew little or nothing but was willing to confess his ignorance, they were unaware of their ignorance or were in the business of pretending to be what they were not. Hence, he knew more than they did, because he knew at least how limited his knowledge was. *This*, he maintained, was the meaning of a pronouncement about him given by the Delphic oracle, which declared him to be the wisest man in the world.

According to Socrates, what Apollo, the god of Delphi, meant when he declared him the wisest man was this: true wisdom belongs *only* to God, and any person who claims to have wisdom and to understand the world is either a fool, a madman, or a scoundrel. The only wisdom accessible to us is the ability to turn the eye of the soul inwards in order to examine ourselves, recognize our limitations, and live a virtuous life. All the rest is sheer nonsense.

Socrates' style of life, his disregard for the opinions of most people, his unrelenting questioning of the moral values of his society, his unwillingness to let himself be coerced by the authorities, the magnetism of his personality, the bluntness and irony with which he dealt with those who pretended to be wise, his uneasiness with religious myths and beliefs, his disdainful attitude toward men in power, his impatience and intransigence in the presence of humbug—whether political, social, philosophical, or religious—all these characteristics and traits were eventually responsible for the trial to which he was subjected in 399 B.C., when he was already a seventy-year-old man. He was found guilty of crimes against the State, specifically of atheism and corrupting the Athenian youth, and was sentenced to death.

In the absence of any writings attributable to him, our information about Socrates comes from the writings of others, some who knew him (primary sources), and others who wrote about him in later times (secondary sources). The main primary sources are Aristophanes, Xenophon, and Plato. Aristophanes, as we have seen, wrote a comedy in which the main character seems to have been drawn closely in accordance with the playwright's own conception of the philosopher. In it, what we find is a strange man who lives in a hanging basket and who speaks a great deal of nonsense to a devoted troop of followers who are as confused as their master. Like Thales and other philosophers, he talks about the earth and the sky and makes all kinds of ridiculous claims about the world. Worse still, he displays no regard for the laws or for moral values and teaches his disciples what amounts to lessons in the art of deception. He gives instruction in how to make the worse argument appear to be the better and to make appearance and reality indistinguishable. Nothing is true and nothing is false, and right and wrong are words that stand for nothing at all. Even belief in the gods is nonsense. In him, then, we come upon a focal point on which various ideas converge, for instance, atheism (the gods are human inventions), ethical nihilism (moral values are senseless rules of conduct that should be ignored), and skepticism (understood in the sense of the denial of the possibility of knowledge).

This portrayal of Socrates includes, we suspect, much distortion and exaggeration. It appears that the playwright used the name of Socrates as a vehicle for the expression of his own ideas and as a means to convey this ideological message: there are no redeeming features in philosophy, for it is nothing but an activity that disorganizes and corrupts the minds of ordinary and law-abiding citizens. In this light, Socrates must have appeared as a dangerous madman in the eyes of the thousands of people who attended the performance of the comedy.

In Xenophon's writings, Socrates is described very differently. There, he is an example of righteousness, and a man devoted to the task of giving intellectual and spiritual assistance to those who crossed his path. Endowed with unusual intelligence and independence of mind, Socrates raised questions about human issues, neglecting anything related to the physical world. Neither scientific issues nor mathematics ever aroused his curiosity. According to Xenophon, the only benefit of mathematics for Socrates was its use in teaching us how to count change at the marketplace. An unassuming man unconcerned with wealth or fame, a good father and a loyal citizen, and a helpful friend—that is, in sum, the man who emerges from the testimony of Xenophon, who in his account of Socrates' trial concludes with these words: "And so, in contemplating the man's wisdom and his nobility of character, I find it beyond my power to forget him or, in remembering him, to refrain from praising him." For this reason, Xenophon saw in his execution a travesty of justice and a grave crime.

Compared with Plato's account, that of Xenophon appears superficial, as if it had missed the true significance of Socrates. His portrayal discloses the image of a good and intelligent man but not the portrait of the extraordinary philosopher described by Plato, who recognized in him a mind sufficiently powerful to revolutionize our conception of the world and, in particular, the conduct of our own lives. Beneath these seemingly discordant representations of Socrates, neither of which is probably completely accurate, it is not difficult to discover the outlines of their literary creators. In our descriptions of those with whom we are acquainted, we often reveal much of what we ourselves are. Still, the portrayals of Socrates found in the primary sources—Aristophanes, Xenophon, and Plato, among others —may contain elements of historical truth. It is, however, unquestionable that the significance of Socrates as a philosopher can be best appreciated by allowing Plato to tell us about him, for it takes a mind as perceptive as Plato's to capture the essence of a mind as complex as Socrates'. For the *philosophical* components of the Socratic presence, especially those that have had a lasting influence in the history of ideas, it is Plato to whom we must appeal.

Plato, also an Athenian, was born in 427 B.C. We have evidence that as a young man he was acquainted with Socrates and that in time he became one of his most devoted students. The influence of Socrates dissuaded him from his political and literary ambitions and guided him in the direction of philosophy. The example of Socrates' life, moral earnestness, and clarity of mind had so profound an effect on Plato that the course of his own life was fundamentally altered. For him, as he tells us, Socrates was "the best, wisest and most righteous man" whom he ever knew. After the execution of Socrates, and after several years of travel and study, Plato founded in Athens the Academy, a philosophical school that remained for almost one thousand years an influential center of learning. There, he wrote a number of dialogues, or literary conversations, all of which have been preserved.

In most of them, Socrates, or rather a character named 'Socrates', is assigned the principal role. In them, we find Socrates as a philosopher 'at work' among the Athenians, conversing and arguing about all sorts of issues, questioning his friends and acquaintances, and forcing them to come up with clear definitions of moral concepts. Sometimes he preaches to them and teaches them moral principles that in his view are essential for a good life and repeatedly urges them to follow a path that is contrary to that of most people. On occasion, he entertains them with tales and stories that serve as allegorical means to convey a philosophical point. At other times, he elicits their help in creating plans for the construction of ideal republics, where, unlike in those of the actual world, people may attain their highest potential. In still other contexts, he appears as a 'wrestler' who competes with others in intellectual contests, disputing the meanings of words, arguing about the interpretation of mythological stories, examining the implications and consequences of opinions and actions, and, as a hungry hound (to use his own phrase), sniffing around for any bits of spiritual worth among his contemporaries and unearthing the hidden manifestations of intellectual humbug that abound among people. Unwilling and perhaps unable to leave people alone and mind his own business, the Platonic Socrates pursues everybody around him, as if intent on finding something of great importance.

Some of his conversations end in confusion, as if having achieved nothing. In others, progress seems to have been made and a semblance of clarity is attained. In most of them, however, what we find is a persistent analysis of language and definitions, and a critical examination of everything that has to do with the intellectual and spiritual aspects of human existence. Irony, humor, politeness, delicacy, and moral earnestness are combined in him with a tremendous intellect, and, amid an avalanche of words, he mesmerizes and transfigures those who listen to him. Some, however, react angrily and impatiently as he forces them to examine their superficially accepted 'truths'. Their reaction is made worse by his repeated assertion that he knows nothing and has nothing to teach and that, like his mother who was a midwife, he can only help people give birth to ideas, while he himself remains barren. Like an annoying gadfly, he awakens them and compels them to face the emptiness and disorientation of their lives, insisting that an unexamined life is not worth living. For him, neither wealth nor prestige nor power nor success nor pleasure amounts to anything, as long as the soul is neglected. Unconcerned with the world of appearance that society idealizes, committed to a life of poverty and austerity, and disdainful of the necessity of having to work for a living (his wealthy friends, he admits, take care of his needs), Socrates walks through the crowded streets of Athens and loiters in the noisy marketplace looking for anyone willing to converse with him. As he tells us in Plato's *Euthyphro*, if he were wealthy, he would pay anyone to join him in his quest for understanding.

It is probably impossible to determine how the Platonic Socrates and the historical Socrates stand related to each other. Is the former mostly a dramatic invention of Plato, created for the purpose of expressing his own ideas? Or are there elements in the latter that are reflected in the former? A solution to what has been called the Socratic problem—the problem of determining the historical accuracy of the testimonies about Socrates—is to assume that in all of Plato's writings, particularly in his early dialogues, information about the historical Socrates is plentiful, despite the fact that Plato did use him on many occasions as a mouthpiece for his own views. Throughout the dialogues there are references to Socrates' ideas, physical appearance, style of life, mode of speaking, social relationships, and other aspects of his life and personality that we can assume to be biographically accurate. The characters of Plato's dialogues are generally historical figures about whom we have information from other sources, and in most instances, Plato's depictions of them agree with what is historically known about them. Why, then, should this not also be the case with his portrayal of Socrates?

In the early dialogues, which were written shortly after Socrates' death, and also in parts of other dialogues, what is traditionally associated with his philosophy emerges with great clarity. This is the case in the *Apology*, in which Plato left for us his version of Socrates' speech at his trial. In it, regardless of the rhetorical elements and embellishments added by Plato, what we find is probably an accurate description, not so much of what Socrates actually said, but what, as a person and as a philosopher, he was. His speech may have been different, but his human presence during the trial, as Plato describes it, is in all likelihood a photographic rendition of what he was. Accordingly, we can reconstruct with some confidence the image of Socrates on the basis of dialogues such as the *Apology*, amplifying and refining it by reference to later dialogues, as well as by an appeal to writers such as Xenophon and Aristotle. This image of Socrates can be drawn in terms of several interrelated components that disclose the portrait of a most original and perceptive man, an example of honesty and righteousness, and a man in whose ideas and life we find an authentic embodiment of philosophy. No better example of a philosopher can be found than Socrates. Becoming acquainted with him is like learning to see the world for the first time.

According to Socrates, the first step in our quest for understanding must involve an introspective journey into our own consciousness, for the road that leads to wisdom begins with the realization that before the world is known, we must know who we ourselves are. Thales and other Presocratic philosophers endeavored to solve the mystery of the world and searched for some basic element, such as water, that could furnish us with the key to explain all things. For Socrates, however, that key does not lie in the world of nature or in physical things. Such things are perceived and known through the senses, but who or what is it that perceives and knows them? Who or what is it that allows for knowledge and understanding to be possible? His answer, often couched in metaphorical and poetical language, is as clear as daylight: the mind, the soul, the self, my consciousness. But what do these terms stand for, and what could be the meaning of the ancient maxim "Know thyself" that was inscribed in the temple of Apollo in Delphi, and that is the first step that must be taken in the adventure of philosophy?

Every child begins his journey through life learning about the world by gathering information through his senses. He is aware that he has parents, that he lives in a house, that the sky is blue, that a certain day of the week is Monday, and so on. His consciousness is constituted by the objects of his experiences: he *is* in some sense his parents, his friends, his home, the sky, his playground, in a word, the world around him. At some point, however, he recognizes that *he* and his surroundings are not the same and that a certain name identifies him as a distinct object among objects. When people say that name, he understands that they are calling *him* or talking about *him*. At this point, he may use the third person singular to refer to himself, and instead of saying "I am here" or "I am tired" he may say "Johnny is here" or "Johnny is tired."[1] Eventually, as language allows him to structure his experiences, the grammatical 'I' emerges and, knowing that he is 'Johnny', he says "*I* am here" or "*I* am tired." It is then that the individual consciousness appears, first still enmeshed in the surrounding world and associated with the body, so that the 'I' and the body are indistinguishable. For some people this is as far as the process develops, and this is all that is required to lead a productive life in society.

In some instances, however, the process moves one step further, and the body is recognized as an object among other objects and as material as the rest of them. The person realizes that he knows and experiences his body as he knows and experiences other things, although in a more direct and intimate way. Still, the body remains an object to be known and experienced. Who or what, however, is it that knows and experiences the body and the surrounding world? I touch a table and I can also touch my feet. I see things around me and I can also see my body. At this point, in at least some individuals, a quantum change occurs in the experience of consciousness. Through my senses I am aware of all sorts of things, including my body, but I can also be aware of being aware of such things. In this awareness of awareness, in this reflected consciousness, the self appears for the first time and I succeed in defining myself, not just as a member of a group or as a body that senses

---

1. Herodotus, the Greek historian, tells us about a tribe in northern Africa whose members had no proper names. Everyone in the tribe was simply known as 'this one' or 'that one'. Among them, the individual consciousness that allows a person to identify himself did not exist.

the world but as a self that is different from what it senses. In Plato's *Phaedo*, there is a passage that gives us a hint concerning Socrates' awareness of the self. When asked by his friends how he wished them to dispose of his body after the execution, he replied that this was inconsequential to him, because whether burned or buried, it was not his self that would be burned or buried but only his body.

The word for 'self' used by Plato is *psyche*, from which words such as '*psych*ology' and '*psych*iatry' are derived, and which we translate as 'mind' or 'soul'. How Socrates understood the relationship between the self and the body is a question that cannot be answered definitely. In some of Plato's dialogues, Socrates conceives of the self as different from the body and, unlike the body, as immortal. Death is a process that only affects the body, and so, what I am will remain in existence after my death. In Xenophon's account, however, there are no indications that Socrates believed in the immortality of the soul, and death is viewed as the destruction of the self *and* the body. Still, whether immortal or mortal, spiritual or material, it is the self or the soul where the essence of the person resides, and it is there that we find the source of consciousness through which we become aware of the world and of ourselves. We are what we are because of the self that lives hidden in us. It is what distinguishes us from one another, from animals (in whom presumably there is no self), and from things.

The question is, however, how can we know the self. Obviously, a name, an age, an appearance, physical features, titles, and similar things cannot provide the answer, because they are either social inventions of no consequence or mere transitory physical states. Again, it is neither by experiencing the world nor our bodies that we can begin the search. A turning of our glance inwards, that is, an introspective examination, is necessary. But how is this to be accomplished? The subject of Socrates' conversations helps us answer this question. He talked almost exclusively about moral issues. In Plato's *Apology*, we hear him say to the jury that he has never had any interest in knowing about the world at large or about scientific matters, because his only concern has always been the examination of moral values, his own and those of others. He insists that those who accuse him of talking about the earth and the sky, or about the nature of the universe, are falsely accusing him. Again, in the *Phaedrus*, another dialogue of Plato, Socrates hurries away from the countryside where he has been spending time with a friend, saying that his only business is in the city, because it is there that people live and where he can converse with them.

This preoccupation with moral concerns is rooted in his conviction that it is only in their context that the self discloses itself. We are what we are because of our moral values and because of the kind of life that we choose for ourselves. Neither in what we own nor in our place in society nor in our physical appearance nor in what we know are we truly what we are, for those things are trappings behind which we often hide ourselves. If the self is to be revealed and if it is to be successfully subjected to examination, we must begin by clarifying the meanings of the values that guide our actions. In absolute honesty and aiming at the greatest clarity, we must answer questions about notions such as righteousness, goodness, virtue, piety, happiness, and justice. We will discover how confused and misguided we are about them and how little we understand them. We will then begin to appreciate the moral dislocation that permeates our individual lives and the societies to which we belong. Our souls, through the examination of our values and of the ways in which we conduct ourselves, will be slowly and painfully peeled off, as the core of an onion when we remove its covering, for a human being is the inner fabric that determines his moral values and his behavior. Nothing else matters. If so, why should have Socrates been interested in other things?

The domain of moral values, however, is one in which the person does not exist by himself as a solitary island in the middle of the ocean. To be human is to be enmeshed in a network of relationships, and every aspect of a person's life is what it is by virtue of the social interactions that make it possible. The self is, therefore, definable in terms of a series of social and political functions that sustain it and determine its nature. Thus, the presence of other selves and the ways in which we are related to them structure what we are. For this reason, moral ideas have no meaning if the person is an isolated individual, which is a virtual impossibility, as Aristotle observed when he insisted that every human being is by nature a political or social animal, and that to be otherwise he would have to be either a god or a beast. When the unavoidable unpleasantness of social existence leads us to Sartre's conclusion that "hell is other people," or when, as in the instance of Thoreau, we may have to seek the seclusion of some Walden and avoid human companionship, even then the presence of the human world remains alive in us, if nothing else in the language that as a *social* reality we carry with us wherever we go. Socrates understood this fact perfectly well. In a passage from Xenophon, he says that he cannot remember a time in his life when he was not in love with somebody, by which he meant that he had spent his whole life looking for companions to join him in the adventure of philosophy. By himself and in the isolation of those Oriental sages who seek wisdom on some deserted mountaintop, Socrates could not have been able to function as a philosopher. Why? Because every imaginable moral idea has meaning only if it involves a human relationship. Alone and by myself, I cannot be either good or bad, just or unjust, honest or dishonest, kind or unkind, and my actions cannot be either right or wrong. I can only be good or bad as a father, a mother, a son, a daughter, a husband, a wife, a neighbor, an employer, a friend, an enemy, a citizen, a teacher, a student, and so on. Each one of these terms entails a relationship between my self and another self or other selves. If my self or my soul (*psyche*) is defined only in terms of my moral convictions, then it is necessary to take into account the other selves that share my world, because in their absence, those convictions would be meaningless. If hell is other people, the search for my self must involve that hell.

Moral convictions are expressed in language, as are in fact *all* ideas. Language is the framework that makes thought possible and is the basis of rationality. Without language it is impossible to think or to reason, which explains why only when a child develops his ability to speak is he able to make sense of things. Language furnishes us with the tool to identify experiences with names and to coordinate them by means of concepts. Words are like memory bytes that allow us to retain and organize our experiences. Without some form of language, therefore, we would remain on the level of simple sense experience and the world would be for us a collection of fleeting impressions. The gift of speech, as Aristotle observed, is what distinguishes us from other living beings and is the prerequisite for any kind of mental activity. The elusive self that stands as the goal of Socrates' search is, therefore, structured in language and cannot be revealed in any other way except through language. As a young man once approached Socrates, he, looking intently at him, said, "Speak, so that I can see you." Merely looking at him was not sufficient. The youth had to open his mouth to let his self come out, and this was possible only as he verbalized what was inside of him, on the tenuous assumption that his words were spoken in absolute honesty. For when, as is often the case, language is used to deceive and misguide, what we accomplish is to hide and distort the self. This misuse of language, as Socrates notes in the *Phaedo*, not only presents a false picture of ourselves but infects the soul with great evil. The liar who uses words to make things appear other than they are, the politician who dupes the masses with euphemisms and empty slogans, and even the ordinary person who speaks for the sake of speaking and who spends his time in idle talk and gossip—all these people misuse language and cover their selves and those of others under thick mantles of falsehood.

The adventure of philosophy initially assumed for Socrates the form of a linguistic analysis of what he and others *said* about moral matters. We say initially, because it is important to bear in mind that for him, language analysis is not the goal of philosophy and should not be viewed as an end in itself. For him, it was only a means, a method, that allowed for the clarification of what he viewed as the essence of human existence. To analyze language for the sake of analyzing language and, worse still, to do it to impress others with our linguistic expertise would have been for Socrates an exercise in idle talk, and not a very exciting one. With him, language analysis has something in common with medicine, for whereas the latter aims at curing the body and preventing disease, the former, if carefully administered, heals the soul of its confusion and sets it on its way to intellectual and spiritual recovery.

What, then, is the language analysis that Socrates proposes as a cure? It has little to do with written language, for this does not let us question those who have written what we read, for which reason Socrates neither wrote anything nor was particularly fond of reading. It has to do with live conversations in which we engage others in the practice of what the Greeks called *parrhesia*, that is, the willingness to 'say it all', not in long and flowery speeches, which Socrates says he had difficulty following and understanding, but in the form of a linguistic exchange known as the elenchus. In Greek, the word *elenchos* refers to what a prosecutor does as he questions a defendant or a witness for the purpose of getting to the truth. It is, then, a form of interrogation in which our interlocutor responds briefly to our questions with a yes or a no, or some short phrase. Eventually, the elenchical process forces him to 'say it all', that is, to speak the truth, at which point his confusion is laid bare and he is compelled to confess his ignorance.

The specific mode of questioning employed by Socrates, the elenchus, proceeds at first by eliciting from the interlocutor some comment involving a moral idea. In the *Euthyphro*, for instance, we begin with the idea of piety or reverence toward the gods, which was among the Greeks equivalent to our notion of right-eousness, for what was in accordance with the will of the gods was the right thing to do. A man named Euthyphro has decided to accuse his father of the murder of a servant. Euthyphro is a religious man who claims to have superior knowledge about piety and matters concerning the gods. When asked by Socrates how he could even think of accusing his father, he replies that his choice is in accord with piety: it is the pious or right thing to do. But how does he justify his decision? Why is accusing his father the right thing to do? At this point the elenchus begins, and Socrates asks Euthyphro to *define* piety. If he is unable to define it precisely, the basis on which he justifies his action is lacking or at best poorly understood.

After a tortuous path of questions and answers, in which each one of Euthyphro's definitions is shown to be unacceptable, he is forced to realize, much to his embarrassment, that he does not understand what piety is. Like most people, he speaks nonsense about all sorts of things, pretending to know what he does not know and falsely claiming to be wise. He is ignorant, and in accusing his father, he acts, again like most people, in a state of ignorance. Socrates, as he ironically tells Euthyphro, is also ignorant, and in asking questions about the meaning of piety, he presumably only wants to gain some knowledge for himself. The truth is, however, that his questions only had the purpose of making Euthyphro recognize his ignorance and empty his cluttered mind in the expectation that his true self, his soul, might rise to the surface. For Socrates, the greatest obstacle on the road to understanding is the unwillingness to come face to face with our lack of under-standing. Only he who is able and willing to confess his ignorance can expect to make intellectual and spiritual progress.

Socrates' confession of ignorance can be understood in a double sense. There were probably many things about which he had little or no knowledge, as in the case of other people, but in his case, he had the honesty and the courage to admit his ignorance. The commitment to the truth about ourselves is an indispensable requirement, and anything else can only serve to bury it even deeper under the appearance of things. His confession of ignorance, however, can also be interpreted as a pedagogical device that helped him accomplish his goal. As noted earlier, his mother was a midwife—a woman who assists other women in the process of giving birth. Like her, then, he, claiming to have no firm ideas in his mind, engaged people in conversations about moral issues, hoping to elicit from them some clear idea or thought. In this sense he was a midwife, for in his presence and through his method others could 'give birth' to ideas while he remained apparently barren.

His questioning was, therefore, a true exercise in *education*, a word that is derived from the Latin *educare*, which means 'to draw or take out'. He could have imparted knowledge or injected ideas into the minds of others, which is what often passes for education. *This*, however, was not what Socrates did. In his view, people have the ability to think clearly and conceive meaningful ideas, because there is in them an inner core, the self or the soul, that constitutes their humanity. Societal influences, linguistic confusions, intellectual laziness, bad choices, unnatural desires, and other inevitable aspects of human life often bury the self beneath deceptions and appearances that prevent us from seeing things as they are and obscure reality in and around us. To use an image from Plato's *Republic*, we could say that people live as if they were chained to the bottom of a dark cave where they see only indistinct shadows that they mistake for reality. This explains why so many human lives are morally and intellectually misguided. How else can we explain the undeniable fact that human communities, past and present, have been and are, to use Plato's words, "almost beyond repair"? Why does human behavior, among individuals and nations, exhibit so much irrationality and senselessness? Why the evil that characterizes so many human actions? Socrates' answer to this question is that evil is the consequence of ignorance, for nobody ever does evil knowingly.

This answer is perplexing, for we can cite instances of human behavior in which evil deeds are done with full knowledge of their evil character. We can recall moments when we have recognized that a certain action is wrong or that the object of our desires is morally unacceptable, and yet we have pursued that action or gone after that object. People do evil things knowingly perfectly well that what they do is evil, for which reason when they are judged by the State, or when society condemns them, they are held responsible for what they have done. In fact, both legally and morally we tend to exonerate a person from guilt when we are certain that he has done wrong in a state of ignorance. From Socrates' perspective, however, *all* evil deeds are without exception the result of ignorance. We choose evil because we fail to recognize its character, and we become involved in wrong-doing only because we are unable to realize that our actions are wrong. Like children who do what they do without thinking, we act blindly and impulsively without understanding the nature and consequences of our actions. As if in a state of intoxication, we fall into modes of behavior that, if our minds were clear, we would not have chosen. Thus, the murderer, the torturer, the thief, the deceiver, the abuser, and all those who lend justification to Schopenhauer's conclusion that "human life must be some kind of a mistake," act as they do because they do not know better. At least during the commission of their evil deeds, their minds have been obscured. This conviction is central to Socrates' philosophy. It provides for us the key to understand the urgency with which he sought to clear the minds of people of their confusions.

Aside from Plato and a few others, however, there have not been many philosophers who have felt comfortable with Socrates' view of the matter, for, as Aristotle observed, it seems to contradict the facts of experience. Who has not confronted the choice between right and wrong, and has not opted, apparently with full knowledge, for the latter? The religious concept of sin, so important in Judaism and Christianity, entails a conscious choice of what is evil. Sin is defined as the commission of a bad action with complete awareness of its character, for which reason neither children nor animals can be guilty of a sin. Yet, for Socrates, nobody can ever commit a sin, because evil deeds are done in ignorance and as a result of ignorance. What underlies this perspective is a sort of intellectual optimism, that is, the belief in the absolute sufficiency of reason as a determining factor in human behavior. It maintains that nobody is capable of doing knowingly anything morally wrong and that once we recognize that a course of action is right, it is impossible for us to do otherwise. It denies that emotions can overrule what the mind commands and declares that a clear mind is the cure for all the moral ailments that afflict people, individually and collectively. According to it, to know the good is to do the good, and not to know the good is a condition that leads to evil or at least to random behavior.

The problem, however, is to understand what Socrates meant by the knowledge that is sufficient to compel us to act only in accordance with that knowledge. Likewise, in saying that evil is the result of ignorance, what did he mean by evil and ignorance? Evil is a concept about which philosophers have expressed different ideas and the definition of which remains controversial. Still, it is not difficult to give clear examples of evil. A concentration camp scene in which we witness killing and suffering cannot be referred to as exhibiting anything else but evil. But with respect to the ignorance that, according to Socrates, leads to evil, what can we say? What is it that the evil person fails to know when he does evil deeds? Again, what is the knowledge that makes the commission of evil impossible? What knowledge is missing from those who do evil deeds?

Obviously, neither the knowledge nor the ignorance that Socrates had in mind is what we generally mean when we use these terms. Knowledgeable people are sometimes evil and ignorant people are sometimes good, and education, at least in the sense in which it is normally understood, does not necessarily promote either a morally good character or a clear mind, and instances of educated people who are morally perverse or intellectually dense are plentiful. As Kant noted, it is sometimes among the ignorant, the uneducated, that we come upon examples of moral worth and a clear mind. This remarkable philosopher, to whom we owe many influential insights in philosophy and in science, and about whom much will be said in the following chapter, was well acquainted with the finest intellects of his time. His parents had only the minimal education that working people in his native Konigsberg were expected to have. Yet, biographers tell us that once he remarked that of *all* the people whom he had known, *they*, his uneducated parents, exhibited the greatest knowledge and exemplified the worthiest style of life. But how could this be? Could people who knew hardly how to read surpass others in knowledge and in moral character?

Something similar is recounted about Socrates. The Delphic oracle, as we have seen, declared him to be the wisest man in the world. Whatever its historical basis may be, this story is instructive, for we learn from it that, as he tells us in Plato's *Apology*, when he heard from a friend what the oracle had said about him, he was perplexed. He knew how little he knew. Then, as if wishing to test the truth of the oracle, he approached various people to find out if anyone knew more than he knew. He questioned theologians and priests, politicians and public figures, poets and orators, philosophers and men of science, and without exception he discovered that while they *thought* that they knew a great deal and were proud of their knowledge, in reality they were as ignorant as he was. His questioning had succeeded in unmasking their intellectual vacuity and moral perversion. Finally, he approached the workers, people who, like his father and like himself when he was young, worked with their hands. Among them, he found more knowledge than among the others, except that in them he also found the tendency of *pretending* to know more than they actually knew, for which reason they were also ignorant, but not as ignorant as the others. Still, somehow they surpassed the apparently learned and sophisticated Athenians. But again, how could this be? Who among the working classes could surpass Anaxagoras' knowledge of the world? Who could rival the theologians in knowing the 'truth' about the gods?

The answer is simply that true knowledge is not found in knowing about the world and that true ignorance—the ignorance that generates evil—is not identical to our lack of information about the world. Knowledge in the sense of *episteme*, that is, information, is an asset that may assist us in coping with experience and with the demands of social existence but that, by itself, is inconsequential and often detrimental, because it can create the impression of true knowledge and can make us oblivious of the knowledge that truly matters. The acquisition of information can become a trivia game that leads nowhere. Our minds may be filled with bits of knowledge about what surrounds us but may remain disoriented and lost. The only knowledge that matters—the knowledge of our selves—emerges in the rigorous examination of moral concepts, in the analysis of ethical terms, and in the review of choices that have moral significance. It cannot be taught nor can it be learned in books or from what others say. It has to come from within ourselves. It is in the context of this knowledge that Socrates maintained that an unexamined life is not worth living.

We come now to the final point of Socrates' philosophy, where the meaning of his ideas and the example of his life converge. In him, thought and action formed an indivisible unity. From the sources, especially Xenophon and Plato, and from his influence on philosophical currents of ancient times such as Cynicism, it is clear that Socrates lived precisely as he thought. In him, then, theory and practice were one. Nietzsche tells us that a true philosopher is one whose convictions can be seen in every one of his words and actions, even in the way he walks. This was apparently the case with Socrates. Every word, every gesture, every action of his revealed with unmistakable clarity his mind and the purpose that structured his life. Before his trial, a famous Athenian orator named Lysias offered him a speech for his defense. Lysias, a writer of forensic speeches, knew perfectly well what Socrates needed to say and what the jurors wanted to hear from him, and assured him that in this way a swift acquittal would be secured. Socrates, however, dismissed the idea and said that he did not need to prepare a speech, *because his entire life had been the preparation for his trial.* His life, then, had been an embodiment of his thought, and the example of his life was there in the open for anyone to see.

Socrates' life was guided by a set purpose and by firm convictions. Among these, as we have seen, was the belief that philosophy should ignore the world at large and concentrate its attention on issues related to human existence. Only in the self can we expect to find the key that opens the door that leads to true knowledge. This self exists and reveals itself in the context of moral values, for which reason Socrates spared no effort in dissecting and examining those values. There was also in him the belief that human problems, both personal and social, are rooted in the lack of clarity of mind, a belief that he expressed in statements such as "evil is the result of ignorance" and "to know the good is to do the good." Other convictions emerge from the sources, as when we hear him insisting that it is better to suffer evil than to do evil, a conviction that runs contrary to what most people are willing even to entertain. Who would choose to be hurt by others rather than to hurt others? Who, when struck on the cheek, would offer the other cheek instead of striking back? We find him likewise *preaching* and *practicing* certain modes of life that stand in opposition to what most people find valuable: poverty rather than wealth, simplicity rather than opulence, austerity rather than indulgence, humility rather than pride, abstinence rather than excessive pleasure, independence of judgment rather than the acceptance of the opinions of the many, and death rather than a life with no moral substance. These convictions set him apart from other people, almost as if he were a living refutation of the values that the social world (his and ours) enthrones as the standard. To the idiocy and senselessness of the social and political world, he opposed a commitment to reason, and to the deceptions and illusions of people's lives he opposed an exemplary attachment to clarity of mind and to 'saying it all'. He was, as Plato tells us in the *Republic*, like "a man who has fallen among wild beasts, and who is unwilling to share in their misdeeds, and is unable to hold out singly against their savagery." We should not be surprised, therefore, that he was at last silenced by the State, for his presence was a reminder that the things that people cherish and seek are not worth very much and that their search for meaning and happiness is misguided. *His* search for meaning and happiness assumed a different direction, one that ran contrary to that of the multitude. If there is anything definite that we can say about him it is that his life was dominated by a relentless search for the human self.

In some sense, we can call Socrates a personification of skepticism. In ordinary speech, when we use this term what we have in mind is a person who is doubtful about what he sees and hears, and who is not convinced by what others say. In a philosophical sense, skepticism denotes a view that denies the possibility of absolute knowledge: nothing can ever be known with certainty. Pyrrho, about whom we spoke in chapter 1, provides an example of this sort of skepticism. During Socrates' time, there were certain philosophers known as the Sophists,[2] who assumed a similar position. Gorgias of Leontini, for instance, maintained that nothing can be known and that, even if it could be known, it could not be communicated through language. With respect to the world and with respect to our own selves, nothing can ever be clarified, and we are condemned to grope in the dark amid appearances, illusions, and shadows. Another example is Thrasymachus of Chalcedon, who appears prominently in Plato's *Republic* and in whom skepticism assumed an uncompromising rejection of *any* knowledge concerning moral values.

---

2. The term 'Sophist' (with a capital 's') should be distinguished from the term 'sophist'. While the former generally refers to a group of philosophers of Socrates' time known for their expertise in the use of language and for their radical skepticism, the latter is a term that includes anyone who possesses (or claims to possess) wisdom (*sophia*).

Terms such as 'good', 'bad', 'right', and 'wrong' had no meaning for him, except as words used for expediency in the *game* of life. Ultimately, then, nothing is morally right and nothing is morally wrong, and human life turns out to be a series of maneuvers in which the only purpose for the individual is to take advantage of others. His philosophy is a clear instance of ethical nihilism.

The skepticism that we can associate with Socrates differs both from what in ordinary speech is meant by this term and from its philosophical meaning. With him, skepticism took on its genuine etymological significance. The word 'skeptic' is a derivation from the Greek verb *skeptomai,* which means 'to look about' or 'to search', and by extension 'to examine'. A skeptical person in *this* sense is neither one who merely doubts what others say nor one who denies that knowledge or reliable information can be obtained but a person who searches and examines. If we become aware that we are missing an important object, we begin to search for it only if we assume that the object still exists somewhere and that it is possible to find it. Otherwise, our search would not make sense. Who would look for something that cannot be found? The search for meaning, especially in the context of moral values, is undoubtedly the commitment that gave Socrates' life its structure and direction. All his activities, his conversations, his choices, and possibly even the most insignificant of his gestures were determined by the purpose that he set for his life, which was to understand the human self both in himself and in others, convinced that *that* understanding is attainable and that it is a necessary requirement for a good and happy life. Whether while in this world he ever attained his goal remains an unanswered question. Let us remember what we said at the end of chapter 1: at the conclusion of his trial, he told the jurors that the prospect of death did not distress him, because his expectation was to go on with the search to which he had devoted himself while alive. In another world, if such a world exists, he hoped to continue his mission. Even among the gods and heroes of the world beyond, his questioning would remain unabated. And so it is among us. Twenty-four hundred years have elapsed since he drank the fatal hemlock, and yet his method, the elenchus, remains among us the most fruitful approach in the search for truth. His questions still have not been finally answered, and we are in many respects as confused as the baffled interlocutors who conversed with him. But his spirit as a philosopher, that is, as a searcher for wisdom, remains alive.

# The Search for Moral Values

Early in his life, every child learns to identify things, people, and situations by using terms such as 'good' and 'bad'. At first, through parental guidance and through the influence of other external factors, his world is divided into three spheres: good things, bad things, and things that are neither good nor bad. Certain kinds of food are good, while others are bad, and some people are recognized as good and others as bad. In every fairy tale, in every story, there is always a good character and a bad character—Sleeping Beauty and the wicked witch, the three little pigs and the big bad wolf, Batman and the Penguin, the 'good guys' and the 'bad guys'. Later on, he learns that some actions are right and acceptable, while others are wrong and unacceptable. Eventually, he becomes aware that there are things that he should do while there are others that he should not do, until, in time, parents and society succeed in creating in him a social conscience, which becomes a judicial authority for determining what is right and wrong, and which, when internalized, becomes *his* personal conscience. If subjected to religious training, the child has still other moral powers over his conduct: God, the teachings of the Bible, the laws of the Church, or the norms prescribed by religious authorities. In all this development what we witness is the formation of his moral ideas.

Since the time of Socrates, the exploration of the meaning, basis, and implications of such ideas has occupied an important place in philosophy, and practically every major philosopher has addressed them in some form or another. We saw in the previous chapter how Socrates sought to understand the human self through the examination of moral values, and how, from his point of view, there was nothing as urgent as sorting them out and reaching clear conclusions about them. We also saw how he attempted to find a rational basis that would set them apart from mere opinions about what is right and wrong. That is what philosophers have endeavored to do after him, giving rise thereby to many theories and views that define and justify the same terms that a child learns early in his life. These theories and views are varied and generally have only one common denominator, which is the assumption that it is through rational analysis that moral issues can be clarified and securely established. This assumption is the underlying theme that has accompanied all philosophical efforts to shed light on the nature of reality and on the significance of human existence.

The word 'ethics' is derived from the Greek word *ethos*, which conveys the idea of customs or habits. The Latin word *mos*, from which the word 'morality' comes, is equivalent to *ethos*, and thus 'ethics' and 'morality' are etymologically related.[1] The custom of the Persians that allowed a man to have several wives was their *ethos*, as was the practice of monogamy among the Greeks. The toleration of incest among certain Egyptian classes was also their *ethos*, and so was the Greeks' prohibition of incest. Even the ways of dressing and eating of various peoples were designated by the same word. Among the Greeks themselves there were examples of *ethos* that distinguished one group from another. In Sparta, the custom was to dispose of deformed children at birth, whereas among the Athenians that custom appears to have been rare. Stealing was an acceptable practice among young Spartans, but among the Athenians, it was viewed as a reprehensible act. In certain ancient cultures it was customary to stone adulterous women to death, but the Greeks would have found this practice absurd. We ourselves are aware of the differences that exist among ethnic, religious, and national groups with respect to customs, and we know that there is probably no practice or habit, no matter how unacceptable or bizarre it may appear to us, that has not been condoned in other cultures. Almost as with the choice of food, moral diversity is a fact that cannot be denied, because the customs of people are as numerous as there are social and cultural groups. Thus, what is customary in one place is unacceptable in another, and words such as 'good', 'bad', 'right', and 'wrong' mean different things in different cultures. It does not require much sophistication to realize that the way in which we live is not the way in which others have lived and live. Cultural relativism, the anthropological and sociological *fact* that moral values vary from culture to culture, is a reality that cannot be contested. The diversity of social conditions, religious beliefs, historical traditions, and other factors have created the variety of moral values that has characterized every historical time. There are as many kinds of *ethos* as there are cultural or *ethnic* groups.

Cultural relativism is, accordingly, a *de facto* human reality. When we speak of something being *de facto*, we refer to the way it *is*. If in a certain culture

---

1. Throughout this chapter I have chosen to use the words 'ethical' and 'moral' as if they were interchangeable. The etymology of these words lends some justification to my choice.

the custom is to abandon one's parents to die when they are old, we would say that in that culture aged parents are *de facto* treated in that way. In ethics, however, a question arises concerning *de facto* conditions. Is the fact that aged parents *are* abandoned a sufficient reason to say that they *ought* to be abandoned? In other words, does the fact that certain customs or practices are *accepted* provide enough justification for saying that they are *acceptable* or morally right? Is there no gap that separates what *is* accepted from what *should* be accepted? Can we convert cultural relativism into ethical relativism, and say, as Ruth Benedict and other modern anthropologists insist, that whatever is normal or customary is what is right, and whatever is abnormal or deviant is wrong? When we introduce terms such as 'right' or 'wrong', we move onto a level known as *de jure* language. The phrase *de jure* (from the Latin word *ius*, from which we derive words such as 'justice' and 'jurist') conveys the sense that something ought or ought not to be. Thus, for instance, when we say that aged parents ought to be abandoned or that it is right to abandon them, our language is *de jure* and expresses an ethical judgment that may or may not lend support to the practice of letting parents die alone when they are old. If our *de jure* statement supports that practice because it is the normal way, then we are accepting ethical relativism (what is normal or accepted is ethically right). If, however, it does not support it, then somehow *de facto* conditions are not sufficient to justify a given practice. Even if practices such as killing deformed children or terminating through abortion every woman's third pregnancy were universal, those practices may not be morally justifiable.

Customs and practices are often reflected in the laws by which a society is governed. What is customary becomes legal, and what is legal reinforces customs and practices. Still, just as from a moral point of view we may raise questions about customs, the same questions may be pertinent in the case of the laws. It makes no difference whether laws, written or unwritten, are established by a dictator or a king or by the majority of the people. Whether in monarchies or in democracies, laws are human instruments that serve various purposes, and are as diverse and changeable as customs. Thus, what is legal in a certain community may be illegal in another, and what is legal at one time may turn out to be illegal at some other time. Think, for instance, of the laws that permit the practice of abortion. There are communities where abortion is not illegal but where a few decades earlier it was a crime. Likewise in the case of capital punishment. Since the nineteenth century, laws that allow the State to execute criminals have been repealed in many societies. In such cases and, in fact, in all cases involving the laws, it is possible to separate the legality of an action from its moral content. Does the fact that abortion has been legalized makes that practice morally acceptable? Do the laws determine the morality of human actions? Is it not possible to regard a law as immoral? Can we not conceive of situations in which the laws may command us to do things that are morally wrong? A negative and perplexing answer to these questions is suggested by Socrates in Plato's *Crito*, a dialogue in which we hear about his reasons for rejecting the opportunity to escape from prison and avoid execution. The main reason, he says, is that such is the will of the laws, and what the laws command is *always* the right thing to do. Apparently, no law can be immoral. To Socrates' answer (whether or not we can attribute it to him) we can oppose the conviction that lies at the basis of anarchism. In this radical and seemingly antisocial stance, *all* laws, without exception, are immoral, and our duty is to stand always in opposition to *all* systems of government and to refuse allegiance to any law.

A less extreme position is found in the ideas and actions of countless revolutionaries throughout history, people who have opposed the Establishment and its laws, and who have sometimes sacrificed their lives to uphold moral principles that transcend the domain of legality. In the name of a higher law, they have refused to comply with *specific* laws that, from their point of view, are immoral. Some, for instance, have advocated civil disobedience and have been willing to break the law to bring public consciousness to the realization that certain laws are immoral. Thoreau opposed the law by refusing to pay taxes because of his conviction that the war waged by the Americans against Mexico was immoral. He recognized the gap between legality and morality and chose to act in accordance with the latter. This dichotomy was also recognized by Locke, when he maintained that there are laws that we have not only the right but the moral duty to disobey. The problem is, however, how to identify the basis on which some laws can be morally challenged. What moral principles can we adduce to justify our setting them aside? Conceivably, such principles may prove to be as relative and mutable as the laws themselves, and as varied as people's customs, in which case we would be again in the midst of ethical relativism.

Ethical relativism, a widely held view that appears to be supported by common sense ("In Rome, do as the Romans do"), brings all moral values to the level of the culture and social group in which they are upheld so that it is impossible to pass judgment on them from a point of view foreign or external to the environment in which they are accepted. If we were to encounter a culture where people are executed for using foul language, we would have to shrug our shoulders, disturbing as such a practice may appear to us, and say, "Well, what they do is the right thing for them." *De facto* values (what people accept as norms) and *de jure* values (what should be accepted from a moral point of view) are one and the same thing. In the world of cultural diversity, values are like musical styles: a man beating a drum is musically speaking neither better nor worse than a classical harpsichordist playing a composition by Bach. Both musicians function well or badly *within* their social worlds, but their musical styles are precisely on the same level. Likewise with respect to customs and laws: in all cases, a custom or a law can be assessed for its moral worth *only* within its historical and social context. Just as there are no universal customs, there are no universal values.

There is a common extreme to which ethical relativism can be taken. Suppose that we abandon the culture, the social group, or the laws as points of reference for ethical judgments, and say that they depend only on the *individual*. What *I* regard as right for myself is simply what is right for *me*. Whatever action I choose for myself and deem morally good is what is good, and whatever I consider morally bad is bad. From this point of view, values are reduced to the individual's opinions or sentiments, for he is the highest court that decides on their moral content. Ethical subjectivism, as this view is known, is common especially in societies characterized by a high degree of cultural diversity and in those in which social disorientation is prevalent. When parental and societal authority is weakened, and when social demands pull individuals in discordant directions, children grow up convinced that nobody but themselves can be a judge in moral matters. Likewise, when the grip of religious ideas is released, such matters tend to fall into a state of disarray, because for many people religion is the basis of their morality. If God is dead, as some modern philosophers maintain, or if the teachings of religious authorities are ignored, where could those who structure their conduct by reference to religious beliefs find a guide for moral decisions? For many, if God does not exist, everything is permissible, just as in the absence of the laws nothing would be either legal or illegal. In such a vacuum, good and bad, right and wrong, and other ethical terms become mere expressions of a person's preferences or choices. If *I* think that euthanasia is justified, then it is not morally wrong. If *my* sexual orientation moves me in a certain direction, who is there to say that such a direction is reprehensible? If *I* am inclined to behave in a way that is contrary to what social practices sanction, who or what can stand in my way to dictate to me moral values? Like preferences regarding food and fashion, then, moral values are expressions of a person's inclinations or preferences. Nothing more can be said about them, and discussions about them are only linguistic games about opinions.

Ethical emotivism emphasizes the primacy of emotions as the basis of moral values and argues consistently that *all* ethical statements are fundamentally emotive statements, that is, ways in which we express our emotions. Thus, in ethical emotivism, it is maintained that the statement "capital punishment is wrong" is equivalent to and should be translated into a statement such as "I disapprove of capital punishment" or "I do not feel comfortable with the practice of capital punishment." Emotions and feelings, however, are varied and numerous, and there is nothing stable in them. Even in the same person, they are subject to sudden changes, and what is agreeable or acceptable at some time may be abhorrent or repulsive at another. If, therefore, we insist on translating ethical statements into emotive statements, and say that nothing supports them except the preferences, emotions, or choices of the individual, ethics ceases to be a philosophical concern and becomes a psychological matter. The philosophers' quest for a rational foundation for moral values would then prove to have been an idealistic undertaking of little worth, for *nothing* can be said about values except that the individual is the ultimate source of them. We would find ourselves in the midst of ethical nihilism, a view that maintains that moral values are nothing or *nihil* (a Latin word that means 'nothing'). For the nihilist, good, bad, right, wrong, and other moral notions do not stand for anything.

For some, however, this interpretation of moral values is inadmissible. The idea that values are changeable and transitory leaves them with a sense of frustration. Socrates himself, in opposing the ethical relativism of the Sophists, felt the need to discover some basis on which values could be firmly grounded. But what could this basis be? What higher moral standard could be found other than customs, preferences, and the individual's choices? Could there be a principle or authority by reference to which we could determine moral values, regardless of when or where they are found? Again, to return to a previous example, imagine that forced abortion becomes a practice in all societies and that it meets with the approval of most people. Would that be sufficient to vouch for the positive moral character of that practice? Can we not argue that even if everybody were in favor of forced abortions, such a practice would remain ethically wrong and morally bad? But, again, on what basis? How can we justify values if we are unwilling to equate them with customs or interpret them as expressions of emotions?

Several solutions have been proposed, but, as we will see, they are often in opposition with one another and are satisfactory only from the point of view of their advocates. This circumstance, however, should not discourage us. Philosophy is an adventure in which questions and problems are bound to remain despite all efforts to arrive at answers and solutions, and this is particularly the case with respect to ethics. Our task is to consider them and come to the most adequate view that in the light of reason suggests itself to us. More cannot be expected. We will examine briefly first what appears to be the most generally accepted solution, theistic ethics, in which order and hierarchy are introduced into ethics through an appeal to religious beliefs. We will then comment on several solutions proposed by philosophers. Ethical naturalism (specifically hedonism and utilitarianism), ethical absolutism, and intuitionism will give us the opportunity to explore some significant issues.

We spoke in the previous chapter about the method employed by Socrates in his search for understanding, the elenchus, and how this proceeds by examining the definitions of moral terms. In his conversation with Euthyphro, Socrates extracts from him various definitions of the concept of piety, beginning with an ostensive definition that only points to an instance. Piety, says Euthyphro, is doing what he does, that is, accusing his father of the murder of a servant. Socrates shows him, however, how inadequate this definition is. Different actions can be called pious, and by simply adducing an instance, what distinguishes pious things from other things is not made clear. In defining the word 'table', for example, it is not sufficient to point to a table and say "This is what 'table' means," because we can imagine tables that have little in common with the table to which we are pointing. Likewise in the case of piety: accusing one's father may be an instance of piety but is *not* what piety is. Pious actions are pious because piety makes them so, and, as a common denominator that underlies them, it is piety that confers on them that specific character. What, then, is this common denominator? What is the essence of piety, by virtue of which certain actions are said to be pious? Unless we understand this essence, the idea of piety remains vague. Eventually, Euthyphro is led to the identification of the essence of piety, which he defines as "doing what the gods will," a definition that agrees with the ordinary meaning of piety among the Greeks. The underlying assumption is, of course, that doing what the gods will —that is, what is pious—is what we *ought* to do, which is how Euthyphro justifies his decision to accuse his father.

Here then we have an example of theistic ethics. Piety or, in our language, the right thing to do, is defined in terms of the obligation to obey the will of the gods. We refer to this kind of ethics as theistic, because God (expressed in Greek by the word *theos*) is viewed as the source of piety or righteousness. It makes no difference whether we understand God in a monotheistic sense (God conceived of as one) or in a polytheistic sense (a plurality of gods). In either case, God is the foundation of values, and obeying his commands is the right thing to do. Neither customs nor emotions nor rational arguments nor anything else can take the place of his will in determining morality.

Let us consider a biblical story that is reminiscent of that of Euthyphro and where we come upon another expression of theistic ethics. Abraham, the great patriarch, once faced a predicament that few among us would welcome for ourselves. God, we are told, said to him: "Take now your only son Isaac, whom you love, and go to the land of Moriah, and sacrifice him to me in a burnt offering on a mountain that I shall show you" (Genesis 22:1-14). In obedience, Abraham took Isaac to the appointed place and prepared him for the sacrifice. As he was about to slit the boy's throat, an angel appeared and, pointing to a ram entangled in a nearby thicket, told him that God was only testing his faith. Praising God, Abraham proceeded to sacrifice the unfortunate ram. For his obedience, he was blessed and was promised that his seed would be as numerous as the stars in the sky and the sands of the sea. His faith had been tested, and he had emerged from the ordeal as a man committed to doing God's will.

Surely, we can interpret this story on many levels, and for some people, it has been a source of great spiritual inspiration. From an ethical point of view, however, it raises issues that are worthy of consideration. If we had been able to question Abraham, as Socrates questioned Euthyphro, we would have heard from him the same definition of piety: piety is doing God's will, and that is why he did not hesitate to take Isaac to the mountain for the sacrifice. It was God, he knew, who had commanded him to do so, and God cannot will anything other than what is right. Until the appearance of the angel, we should note, Abraham had no idea that it was only his faith that was being tested and that in the end he would return from the mountain with his unharmed son. Accordingly, as far as he was concerned, God had willed the slaughter of Isaac, and Abraham's own will had become one with God's will. If the moral content of actions resides not only in their commission but in the intention to commit them, then Abraham's *determination* to kill his son, regardless of the reasons and the outcome, is what matters from an ethical point of view. If I intend to poison somebody but I fail, I am morally accountable because of my *intention*. Thus, Abraham was morally accountable, even if he acted in compliance with God's will and even if the outcome was not what he anticipated.

Sometimes we hear of instances in which people have done strange things, because, they say, God has told them to do so. In countless incidents, God's will has been used to justify actions that are often in opposition with one another. God's will, some believe, is that we love one another and respect all forms of life and that we be compassionate with those who suffer. Examples of people who have let their actions manifest *this* will of God are plentiful—one thinks of Saint Francis of Assisi or Mother Teresa of Calcutta. Yet, a glance at human history unveils a more varied scenario. Also in the name of God, people have been persecuted, burned alive, exterminated, and made to suffer on earth what sinners should expect to undergo in hell—one thinks of the Inquisition and of the holy wars that have plagued so many lands. Sometimes even within the same religion and based on the same sacred scripture, different and contradictory types of behavior and moral norms have been advocated in the name of God. Monogamy, polygamy, sexual abstinence, chastity, human sacrifice, the love of one's enemies, the extermination of heretics and infidels, and other things—all have paraded at some time or another, and even at the same time, as divine commands, and what is sinful at some time becomes permissible at another. One might conclude that God does not always speak clearly or that his will is not always the same or, what is more probable, that those who 'hear' his voice or interpret his messages are as bewildered as the confused Euthyphro. How, except in a leap of faith, can we presume to know that it was God's voice that Abraham heard? Could he have been mistaken? How, then, can God's will serve as the basis of moral values if it is as relative and unpredictable as the emotions and opinions of those who pretend to know it and as difficult to decipher as the greatest mystery? Does not theistic ethics leave us in the same impasse as ethical relativism and ethical subjectivism? How can we rely on something about which opinions are varied and changeable and about which, unless we are endowed with faith, there is nothing we can say with assurance?

Furthermore, as Socrates reminds Euthyphro, we still have to confront the most critical question about theistic ethics. Is what God wills pious or right because he wills it, or does he will it because it is right? If we opt for the former alternative, we face the problem of the multiplicity of beliefs about God's will, which is exhibited in the enormous number of religions found at all times. Each religion teaches something different about God's will and provides its own account of what is moral. If, however, we opt for the latter alternative and say that what God wills is right because it is right, we are left with the problem of determining the essence of righteousness. What is it that God recognizes in certain actions that merits his divine approval? In either case, we have not advanced one inch beyond ethical relativism. Because of this, valuable as theistic ethics may be as a controlling mechanism in human behavior and as a guide for human conduct, it is not a philosophically fruitful approach to moral issues. Besides, for those who deny the existence of God, theistic ethics provides no solution at all. If God proves to be an illusion, the basis of values dissipates into thin air, and everything becomes permissible, which is what ethical nihilism maintains.

Other approaches, therefore, are required if we intend to explore ethics from a philosophical point of view. We will begin to examine some of these with comments about ethical naturalism. Naturalism refers in this context to those conditions and inclinations that are *natural* in human beings and somehow define human *nature*. In ethical naturalism, accordingly, there is no need to appeal to a divine power nor is it necessary to create abstract formulas to discover the basis of ethics. There are several kinds of ethical naturalism, which is understandable given the variety of characteristics that appear to be natural in human beings. Possibly the most common forms are eudaemonism and hedonism. The word eudaemonism comes from the Greek word for 'happiness' (*eudaemonia*). In Greek and in English, the meaning of 'happiness' is complex and evokes various ideas, and who is happy and what are the conditions that lead to happiness are questions that admit of many answers. In Aristotle's writings, *eudaemonia* conveys the sense of 'well-being' or 'fulfillment', and does not denote a life filled with pleasures, possessions, or fame. Neither does it stand for the transient feeling that we express when we say, for example, "I am happy to meet you" or "I am so happy that I did well in this philosophy course." For Aristotle, happiness is not a feeling, an emotion, or a state of mind. If happiness and pleasure were the same, people who experience pleasure would be happy, but the fact is that sometimes they are and sometimes they are not. Likewise with respect to wealth: if wealth and happiness were related, the wealthy would be always happy, but, again, sometimes they are and often they are not. There are rich people who are surrounded by the luxuries and pleasures that others covet and yet who live under an intolerable burden of despair, which shows that wealth does not necessarily lead to happiness. Still, if what is generally identified with happiness is *not* happiness, what could happiness be?

According to Aristotle, happiness is the ultimate purpose of human existence. Just as artifacts are made to fulfill a purpose (a knife is made to cut, a piano to play music, a pen to write, and so on), a human being comes into this world to fulfill a purpose and that purpose is to be happy. Human life has no other purpose. Happiness is the goal of every human action, and whatever we do reflects that goal. We buy a certain house or a certain car because that, we think, will make us happy, and we establish personal relationships because we expect to be happy. We spend years pursuing an education, again because we hope to attain happiness, and few are those who do anything for the express purpose of being unhappy, because it is happiness that by nature most of us desire. And yet, the cruel fact of human life is that there are not many who attain lasting happiness. Schopenhauer may have been correct when he observed that most people live miserable lives, oscillating between boredom and misery, happiness being only a fleeting moment between these two extremes. On the faces of old people, said Schopenhauer, one can always see written in large letters the word DISAPPOINTED, for what they have spent their lives seeking has eluded them. If, however, this is true, where does that leave Aristotle's enthronement of happiness as *the* most natural condition and as *the* goal of human activities? If nature meant for us to be happy, why are we often so miserable?

Aristotle provides an answer. Assuming that happiness is understood as well-being or fulfillment, and not in terms of pleasures and other transient things, the fact that people often fail to attain it is explainable as a result of their lack of mind. Like children in a candy store, who grab and eat whatever comes their way, who follow blindly their appetites, and who go home with a bad case of indigestion, people go through life snatching every sort of pleasure, every object, every pastime, only to find themselves in as much misery and boredom as before, for which reason their quest begins anew with precisely the same results. But why should this be so? Because, Aristotle might say, people, like children, fail to grasp the connections and relationships that exist among things. A moment of pleasure may give the impression of making us happy but may also bring about devastating and lasting consequences both for ourselves and for others. When the feeling of pleasure subsides, however, existential emptiness returns with a vengeance, and then we conclude that what we need is another pleasure, and we undertake once more our misguided quest. Other examples can be adduced. In our age of consumerism, clever advertising creates artificial needs and convinces people that only if they have this or that new product, visit this or that place, experience this or that novel sensation, they will be happy. How many pairs of shoes would make a person happy? How many cars would satisfy us? How much money must we have? The answer is always the same: as many and as much as possible. Yet, we know of people who own thousands of shoes, dozens of cars, and millions of dollars and are still unhappy. What is missing in their lives?

In the light of reason, Aristotle insisted, human activities should be viewed as a network of means and ends. If we act with some dosage of rationality—if we know why we do what we do—everything we do has a goal, a purpose, an end. For instance, why am I taking a philosophy course? Most likely, I might reply, because I want to graduate. However, why do I want to graduate? Probably because I want to get a well-paid job. Why? Because I want to earn money. Why? Because I want to buy all sorts of things and provide for my needs. Again, why do I want such things? Because I hope to be secure and comfortable and live a happy life. Happiness is, then, the goal that guides the sequence of my actions, including my taking this course. Does it make sense, however, to ask why do I want to be happy? *This* question, Aristotle argued, is senseless, because happiness is that for which we do everything and is not something we seek for the sake of anything else. As the most *natural* condition, happiness is the final goal and purpose of human life. Other things are sought for its sake, but it is an end in itself. But if this is so, we must ask again, why are there so many failures in the human quest for happiness? Why the personal and social unhappiness in which so many people live?

Aristotle's answer is that this is due to our inability or unwillingness to understand the hierarchy of means and ends that lead to happiness. We either confuse means with ends or ends with means or fail to realize that many of our actions do not lead to happiness, or have no understanding of what happiness is. Happiness, as the purpose of human life and as the standard of reference by which actions can be judged to be good, bad, or indifferent, is an *activity*, not a feeling or a state of mind, that results from rational choices and is made or created through a conscious effort to discriminate among the things we seek. It entails reason and reflection and aims at the development in ourselves of certain virtues or strengths and at the avoidance of certain vices or excesses. The idea of virtue is expressed in Greek by the word *arete*, the meaning of which is 'strength' or 'excellence', as when we speak of the *virtu*osity of a pianist whose mastery reveals years of disciplined practice. Likewise, the morally virtuous person has the strength (*arete*) to shape his character in a way of life in which certain means lead to certain ends that allow him to attain happiness. His personal *and* social life (like every person, he is a political or social being) conforms to those ideals that are good from the point of view of reason. Should he struggle to own a thousand pairs of shoes? Should he devote his energy to amassing a fortune? Should he spend his time in the pursuit of transitory pleasures? Should he seek to control and manipulate those around him? How senseless, indeed, that would be, because those things do not ensure happiness. Instead of groping in the dark and satiating his whims and desires, he should aim at living an unencumbered style of life in which there is neither excess nor lack regarding the things that make life worth living.

Aristotle's insistence that in happiness we find the basis of moral values is found among many other philosophers. The adherents of Stoicism, for instance, also viewed happiness as the purpose of human life, but in them, as Epictetus maintains, happiness emerges as a state of mind in which, through the use of reason, they succeed in neutralizing feelings and emotions, which are the greatest source of the restlessness in which people live. The Stoics spoke of happiness in terms of what they called *apatheia* (from which we derive the term 'apathy'). To minimize our needs and control our desires, to distinguish those things that can be changed from those that are unalterable, to accept conditions and situations that are unavoidable, to rectify those over which we have control, to recognize the *logos* or reason that governs the universe, and to let our own rationality conform to it—these are ideals that we find stressed in Stoicism. Again, as with Aristotle' ethics, it recognizes in happiness *the* natural condition at which human life aims and explains our failure to come even close to it in terms of the lack of reason that characterizes many human lives.

The disassociation of happiness from pleasure, so important among the Stoics, is *not* what we encounter in hedonism. The Greek word *hedone* stands for words such as 'pleasure' and 'enjoyment', both physical and otherwise. In hedonism, therefore, to be happy and to experience pleasure are one and the same thing. A life deprived of pleasures and immersed in pain cannot be a happy life. According to hedonism, the most natural human tendency is to seek pleasure and avoid pain. We see it in children, who invariably look for things that give them pleasure and shun things that produce pain. Even animals are no different in this respect. As a child learns to use ethical language, it is by reference to pleasure and pain that terms such as 'good' and 'bad' first acquire their meanings. Sweets are good because they are pleasurable, while castor oil is bad because its smell and taste are unpleasant. People, too, are good or bad depending on whether they provide pleasure or pain. What could be more in accordance with human nature than to seek pleasure and avoid pain, and to call the former good and the latter bad? For this reason, psychological hedonism affirms that as a matter of fact every human being seeks pleasure and avoids pain in all his actions. Human behavior is, therefore, explainable in terms of the search for the former and the avoidance of the latter. In whatever we do, we are under the control of these determining factors. Even when pain and suffering are sought, as in masochistic behavior, pleasure is the goal, and, strange as it may seem, the masochist derives pleasure from pain.

Problems soon arise from an ethical point of view as we reflect on psychological hedonism. We face, for instance, the fact already mentioned earlier that pain and suffering, sometimes brought about by nature and sometimes by our own choices, are pervasive human conditions. Furthermore, the experience of pleasure admits of many variations—what pleases someone, causes pain in someone else—and in the same person, what is pleasurable at some point is painful at another. A child finds pleasure in watching cartoons on television, but grown-ups seldom do. Then, too, there are different kinds of pleasure, and the intensity with which pleasure and pain are felt varies from person to person and from culture to culture. In certain cultures, torturing and killing a bull is a source of enjoyment, while in others such a pastime may cause distress and disgust.

But perhaps the most critical issue regarding psychological hedonism is whether it can serve as the basis for moral values. Is it possible to extract from the *de facto* condition that people seek pleasure and shun pain the *de jure* contention that pleasure is what people *ought* to seek and pain what they *ought* to avoid? Stated differently, can we derive ethical hedonism from psychological hedonism? Should pleasure and pain be the standards according to which we pass judgment on the moral content of human actions?

In the eighteenth century, an ethical theory known as utilitarianism was developed by Jeremy Bentham, an English philosopher with considerable influence on the development of the social sciences. His ideas were extended and refined in the nineteenth century by another influential philosopher, John Stuart Mill, to whom we owe many insightful ideas. Although utilitarianism has roots in earlier hedonistic theories, it was Bentham who gave to it its first clear formulation. In his *An Introduction to the Principles of Morals and Legislation*, he states that "Nature has placed mankind under the governance of two sovereign masters, *pain* and *pleasure*. It is for them alone to point out what we ought to do, as well as to determine what we shall do. On the one hand the standard of right and wrong, on the other the chain of causes and effects, are fastened to their throne." Here, psychological hedonism and ethical hedonism converge. As human beings, we *naturally* avoid pain and look for pleasure, and this natural circumstance allows us to affirm that it is pain that we *ought* to avoid and pleasure that we *ought* to pursue. Bentham argues that there is nothing more obvious than the fact that pain and pleasure control human behavior "as two sovereign masters" and that this is sufficient for us to base moral judgments on that fact. What is *de facto* engenders what is *de jure*, and any efforts to find the basis of morality in ideas that transcend human nature are futile dreams of no substance. Furthermore, all attempts to justify values on a basis other than pleasure and pain are either camouflaged manifestations of utilitarianism or the result of superstitions, irrational customs, or mental confusion. Is God not believed to be good because of his design to bring about pleasure for all his creatures? And as for those who speak of reason as the supreme source of moral values and as the standard of right and wrong, are they not, too, advocating the well-being of people as the highest moral goal?

The principle on which utilitarianism is based states (1) that utility is the natural aim at which human actions, personal and collective, are directed, and (2) that, precisely for this reason, utility ought to be the only ethical standard. Nature provides the answer to the question that philosophers have struggled to answer, namely, how are moral judgments justified? The idea of utility, however, must be clearly understood. Utility is anything that brings or is expected to bring about the greatest happiness for the greatest number of people. Happiness in this context, according to Mill, means pleasure and the absence of pain, and, by extension, things like benefit, comfort, advantage, usefulness, joy, and anything that in ordinary speech is associated with words like 'good' and 'well'. On the other side, things that are contrary to utility are those that create unhappiness—pain, fear, anguish, sickness, misery, and everything that we mean when we use words like 'bad' and 'evil'. In utilitarianism, therefore, human actions can be separated into two groups: those that promote utility and those that do not. The former aim at creating the greatest happiness, while the latter produce the opposite effect. The former are morally good, while the latter are bad. The addition of the phrase 'for the greatest number of people' is important, because it establishes the difference between utilitarianism and those forms of hedonism in which the individual is viewed as the only point of reference. It is not *my* happiness, *my* pleasure, *my* utility that utilitarianism postulates as the standard of morality, but the happiness of as many human beings as possible. If utility is understood in terms of those actions and conditions that benefit only the individual in disregard of his social context, we are in the midst of ethical egoism, a common attitude akin to ethical subjectivism, in which the individual is the judge of what is good or bad, right or wrong, which is far from what utilitarianism advocates.

Accordingly, utilitarianism deals with ethics from a social point of view and insists that moral values, no less than the laws by which societies are governed, must be judged by the utility that they promote. Earlier we raised the issue of the relationship between morality and legality, and we said that laws can sometimes be judged to be immoral. Take, for instance, laws that sanction the execution of criminals. Are those laws morally defensible? Can we construct a moral argument by reference to which they may be deemed right or wrong? Utilitarianism answers that as long as we argue from the point of view of utility, the moral content of those laws can be empirically ascertained. Still, how are we to proceed? On the assumption that actions and laws are morally good only if they promote the greatest happiness for the greatest number of people, we can make some progress. Ascertaining whether an action or a law does or does not conform with this assumption is an empirical process in which we examine how an action or a law impacts on people's lives. It is not a matter of arguing from the perspective of innate or inalienable human rights or self-evident principles or rational norms or a biblical commandment or anything of that sort. Independent of their utility, neither actions nor laws are moral or immoral. Thus, if, as Mill himself stated in the British Parliament during a debate on capital punishment, we can empirically show that as a deterrent this practice has a beneficial effect on society at large, and that for the criminal himself, a life in prison is more painful than a quick execution, *then* we will have demonstrated that capital punishment is under certain circumstances a morally acceptable practice. In the balance of happiness and unhappiness, the standard of utility would force us to rescind all moral objections against it. If we can demonstrate that executions accrue more happiness than unhappiness for the greatest number of people, the moral case against capital punishment would have to be closed. And the same can be said with respect to all other laws and actions. Utility is and should be the sole criterion in ethics.

Yet, doubts and questions about utilitarianism abound. We could, for instance, look more closely into the contention that there is nothing intrinsically good or bad, right or wrong in human actions and that it is only in their ascertainable consequences that their moral import resides. Utilitarianism alleges that the intentions responsible for actions are morally neutral. If I undertake an action for the purpose of hurting someone, but I only succeed in augmenting his happiness without diminishing the happiness of anyone else, my action would turn out to be morally good because of its consequences, regardless of my intention. For those for whom, like Kant, moral worth depends at least in part on human intentions, this aspect of utilitarianism makes little sense. Furthermore, even if we grant that in determining moral worth we should look only at the consequences of actions, we still have to deal with the difficulty of ascertaining what the consequences of future actions will be. Can we, as Bentham proposed, develop a scientific pleasure calculus in order to measure utility in terms of qualities such as intensity and duration, and assign to each pleasure or moment of happiness a numerical value? Bentham lived at a time when the social sciences were in their infancy and when there was hope of taking them on a path, similar to that of the natural sciences, that leads to quantification. Just as we can assign a numerical value to the temperature at which water boils ($100°$ C), it was hoped that, through an empirical pleasure calculus, we could determine exactly the numerical value of any pleasure and of happiness itself. Ethics would then become a science just like physics or any other natural science. Instead of saying "I am very happy today," I might say "The present level of my happiness is 30; what is yours?" The effect of actions and laws could eventually be measured with exactitude with respect to their utility, and thus the moral worth of actions and laws would be amenable to precise determination.

The question is, however, whether the complexity of human nature permits us to aim at exact measurement concerning happiness. Pleasures, as Mill conceded, are subjective experiences, and we cannot speak about them as if we were speaking about water or any other physical thing. Moreover, merely quantifying the intensity, duration, and other qualities of pleasure ignores the fact, also recognized by Mill, that some pleasures seem to be morally superior to others. Imagine, for instance, that scratching one's head became the most pleasurable experience for human beings. Would that fact alone be enough to conclude that scratching one's head is the highest moral ideal? Certain pleasures, specifically those that distinguish us from our evolutionary relatives in the animal kingdom, appear to be preferable to others. Struggling with philosophical issues—the highest pleasure among philosophers—is not comparable with what pigs seem to experience when they wallow in mud. Still, why? Mill suggested an answer that should not be dismissed offhand: pleasures can be *vertically* classified in terms of their desirability by people who have experienced them. Only if I have wallowed in mud *and* am acquainted with the pleasures of philosophy can I reach a sensible conclusion as to which is preferable. The music of Mozart and the music of a rock band can only be compared by those who are well acquainted with both, and the fact that the former is appreciated by very few, while the latter is the entertainment of many, is inconsequential in an effort to compare them.

In this attempt to classify pleasures vertically, utilitarianism discloses what from the point of view of its critics is one of its weaknesses. If some pleasures are better than others, regardless of the *amount* of utility that they create, what is it that renders them so? Is there something in them that makes them intrinsically superior? Other perplexities arise as we consider the phrase "the greatest happiness for the greatest number of people," because the greatest number of people would include all present (and perhaps future) human beings. If the welfare of an imperialistic nation is ensured by the exploitation of a small undeveloped nation, does that fact alone render that exploitation morally acceptable? Does the majority have the moral right to enslave a minority of unfortunate people, because in that process the greatest number of people would benefit? Still, these questions pale in comparison with the main question that can be raised about utilitarianism and about other types of ethical naturalism: is the fact that pleasure and happiness *are* the normal goals of human behavior a sufficient reason to conclude that they *should* be our moral goals? Stated differently, is what is *accepted* equivalent to what is *acceptable*? Is there a bridge that allows us to move from facts to moral judgments? Can *de facto* conditions furnish us with the basis for *de jure* statements?

George Edward Moore, a twentieth-century philosopher, mounted a sustained attack on ethical naturalism, and on utilitarianism in particular, because, in his view, we find in them what he called the naturalistic fallacy. A fallacy is a mistake in reasoning or an argument in which the premises do not justify the conclusion. For instance, if after being acquainted with only a few members of a racial group we reach a conclusion about the entire group, we would be committing a fallacy, because generalizations are not logically justified on such a limited basis. Again, if we say that all human beings have hair and are rational, and if we conclude from this statement that all hairy creatures are rational, we would also be guilty of a fallacy. Fallacies, then, are errors in reasoning, which, although common, need to be exposed and corrected. The naturalistic fallacy that Moore discerned in utilitarianism is the belief that from what *is* we can deduce what *ought* to be or that the presence of a *natural* characteristic allows us to construct on that basis a set of moral values. The fact that people desire pleasure does not make pleasure morally desirable. But if natural characteristics do not provide that basis, what can?

For Moore, the answer lies in an approach to ethics known as intuitionism, a view that argues that the moral character of an action is unrelated to its consequences and to the intentions that are responsible for it and is intuited or recognized directly by the mind. The word 'intuition' in this context refers to direct and immediate knowledge, such as, for instance, what registers in the mind when we see a red object and know that it is red. The color of the object is known directly and is not dependent on reasoning or on feelings or emotions about the object. We know or intuit redness when we see it, and in that sense the perception of something red is an intuition. The problem with many attempts to make sense of moral values, Moore argues, is that ethical terms are *defined* in terms of qualities, characteristics, emotions, the will of God, and other similar things. In theistic ethics, we maintain that goodness is obeying God's will, and in ethical relativism, righteousness is what is normal. From the point of view of hedonism, goodness is what causes pleasure, and, from the perspective of utilitarianism, what promotes utility. In all these cases, a definition of a moral quality is proposed. When we define a term like 'triangle', we unpack its meaning by spelling out its components. Thus, we say that a triangle is a closed plane figure with three angles. 'Closed', 'plane figure', and 'three angles' are its components.

In the instance of qualities that are intuited, however, no definitions are possible, because such qualities are simple and have no components. Take the case of redness. How can we define it? The physical definition of the color red furnished in terms of the wavelength of light would leave a blind person unable to grasp what the *perception* of red is. How else, then, could we define it except by pointing to a red object and saying, "This is red"? The color red, therefore, can only be grasped through an intuition, and nothing else can give us even a faint idea of what it is. Intuitionism argues that things are not otherwise in the case of moral qualities. The idea of 'good', for example, is a simple idea that can be recognized only through an intuition. It cannot be broken into components and cannot, therefore, be defined. We cannot say that good is what brings pleasure or happiness or what society finds acceptable or what God commands, because all these statements attempt to define what is undefinable. Moral qualities can only be exemplified, which leads us back to Euthyphro's first definition of piety. When asked by Socrates what piety is, he replies, "Piety is doing what I am now doing, namely, accusing my father." He points to his action and calls it pious, because he has intuited the quality of piety in it. Unencumbered by considerations concerning the basis of his action or its consequences, Euthyphro simply follows his intuition of piety. Could it be that, just as we need the sense of sight, which is common to all human beings and through which we see the color red in an object, we are provided with a moral *sense*, an intuitive capacity, that allows us to recognize the moral content of human actions? Should we not affirm, then, as Wittgenstein did, that ethics is the sort of thing that cannot be explained in language, but can only be directly experienced?

As with utilitarianism, however, there are questions regarding intuitionism. Not the least among them is the fact that whereas we do not often find people arguing about whether an object is red or not, we do find them at odds, indeed sometimes killing one another, about moral issues, because what some recognize as bad, others intuit as good. What some condemn as immoral, others declare to be good. Where, then, is the moral sense, the intuitive capacity, that empowers us to recognize moral qualities? The answer suggested by intuitionism is that the moral sense is always present in human beings, but that, through the influence of senseless traditions and irrational prejudices it is often buried in the conscience or becomes distorted. Children are not aggressive or discriminatory but become so through misguided parental and societal influences that dull their moral sense and their capacity to intuit the good, until they become morally blind. How else can we explain the behavior of executioners in concentration camps except by saying that they were morally blind? Was it the ideological 'uniform' drilled into them that made them blind? How else can we account for the moral mire in which so many people live? Moral qualities may be undefinable and may be grasped only through intuition, but the brutal social fact is that few are those who intuit them and for whom they have any significance. The person who recognizes the good and lives virtuously is probably as rare as the true human being for whom Diogenes searched in vain as he walked the streets of Athens carrying a lighted lamp in daylight. However, if not even intuitionism stands firmly as an adequate ethical theory, are we to concede defeat in our search for a stable basis of morality and say that such a basis cannot be found?

A negative answer to this question comes to us from one of the most perceptive philosophers, Immanuel Kant. In him, we encounter an effort to find a basis of morality that is free from the insecurity and feebleness of ethical naturalism and intuitionism.[2] He developed certain rational principles that could serve as the foundation of morality and could introduce clarity where only vagueness and confusion have prevailed and certainty where only opinions and emotions have been the moral standards. These principles are a priori, that is, strictly rational, not a posteriori or based on experience. Moral values, according to Kant, are *practical* rules of conduct by reference to which we can act morally. In so doing, the will is the determining factor. It is not sufficient, as with Socrates, to *know* what is good to act in a moral way. What is necessary is to *choose* what is good. The idea of *choosing* presupposes that we are free to do so, for which reason Kant insisted that, mysterious as human freedom may be from a theoretical point of view, it must be accepted as an unquestionable reality. If, as affirmed by determinism, actions are always the result of prior conditions and predispositions, moral values are meaningless. No one can be either morally praised or blamed for actions that have not been *freely* chosen. Just as it would be absurd to hold a person accountable for his height or his age, it would be equally absurd to refer to human behavior as good or bad if freedom had not played some part in it. Thus, a free will that is able to make rational choices is a postulate that must be accepted.

Happiness, as we have seen, has often been viewed as fundamental in ethics. According to Kant, however, happiness is unrelated to the content of ethical statements and to moral behavior. We may *hope* that moral choices may lead to happiness, but we cannot *expect* with assurance to be happy by acting in accordance with moral principles, for a virtuous life can sometimes be an unhappy life. When confronting the alternative of having to choose between what is right and what promises to make us happy, morality demands that we choose the former. Happiness, therefore, cannot be the basis of moral values, and the same can be said about pleasure, customs, laws, and what some interpret to be God's will. All these things provide only transitory and relative justifications for various actions and types of behavior, and their relativistic and uncertain nature do not allow us to establish morality on a firm foundation. What is morally good, Kant affirmed, is absolutely independent of such considerations and even of the consequences of our actions. Just as the principles that govern mathematics are unrelated to our feelings and opinions about them, and remain unchanged and universal regardless of what we may say or believe, so are moral laws.

The problem is, however, how to determine their content. If they cannot

---

2. Kant, who died in 1804, anteceded the rise of ethical theories such as utilitarianism, pragmatism, and intuitionism. Still, as has been emphasized throughout this book, there are hardly any ideas or theories in modern philosophy that we can regard as entirely new. Precursors of utilitarianism and intuitionism can be found long before the time of Bentham and Moore.

be learned in experience and are unrelated to happiness, emotions, traditions, social or personal benefit, religious beliefs, and other considerations, what is the basis of the moral law proposed by Kant? What could its source be? Its source, he insisted, is reason, more precisely practical reason, and knowledge about it is thoroughly rational and a priori. There is something in it that is reminiscent of what we mean when we speak about a truth as being 'self-evident', for there is no doubt that its a priori character renders it so. We must 'see' it, not with the physical eyes but through reason, and then we will recognize it as the only foundation of morality.

Kant spoke of the moral law in terms of what he called the categorical imperative. The word 'imperative' conveys the sense of a command, an obligation, or a rule that must be obeyed. In grammar, the phrase "Go to the window and open it" is an imperative that can be contrasted with an assertion or statement of fact such as "The window is closed." The Ten Commandments are examples of imperatives. There are, however, two kinds of imperatives, namely, hypothetical and categorical. A hypothetical imperative is one in which we express the idea that something should be done if we want something else. For instance, "*If* I want to be rich, *then* I must work a great deal" or "*If* I want to be successful, *then* I must abide by society's rules." The presence of the *if-then* relationship makes these statements hypothetical. While common and useful, however, they are relative and uncertain. Not everybody wants to be rich or successful, nor is there any assurance that hard work or complying with social norms lead to wealth or success. For this reason, hypothetical imperatives are useless in ethics, and we must turn our attention to the categorical imperative. The word 'categorical' refers in this sense to a command that is absolute and universal and that admits of no exceptions or extenuating circumstances. It is as absolute and universal as the statement $2 + 2 = 4$. Whether in China or in New York, among the ancient Greeks or among ourselves, on the earth or in another galaxy, two things plus two things yield four things, regardless of how we may feel about the matter. And this is precisely what we need in ethics if we are to realize the Socratic dream of discovering an unshakable foundation for it. Still, what is the categorical imperative in which the moral law is expressed?

This moral law can be understood in terms of the notion of duty, which is the obligation to act in a certain way. Morality requires that we act *always* and under *all* circumstances in accordance with duty and *only* for the sake of duty. Striving to be good because we want to be happy, or because we want to avoid unpleasant consequences, is not morally acceptable. Only when duty is the sole reason why we choose to actualize in ourselves the moral law can we move along the path that leads to moral worth. The guidelines that can lead us along this path are outlined in terms of what Kant called the categorical imperative, which can be expressed in two interrelated maxims. The first assumes this form: Act always as if your actions were to become a universal law (or rule) for all human beings. The second can be stated thus: Treat all human beings (including yourself) as if they were ends in themselves, not means towards an end. In the first, we are told that whenever we undertake an action, we must ask ourselves if that action is the sort of thing that we would propose as a universal rule for all human beings in a situation similar to ours. Suppose that I am tempted to cheat in a philosophy test. Would I want cheating to become the norm for all students? Suppose again that if I am married, I become engaged in unfaithfulness. Would I advocate that sort of behavior for all married persons? Suppose again that a parent abuses or mistreats his child. Would it be desirable for all parents to do likewise? Once more, suppose that I use language to deceive others. Would that be what I recommend for everyone? Cheating, marital unfaithfulness, child abuse, and lying are, therefore, immoral because of the absurdity of proposing them as universal modes of behavior. What is good for me is, therefore, morally right if and only if it can be universalized. A moral value that is relevant only to me or only to any other individual person or group is an absurdity. As Sartre put it, in choosing what I do, I must choose as if I were acting on behalf of humanity.

In the second formulation of the categorical imperative, we are reminded that every human being, regardless of who he or she may be and irrespective of social conditions, racial or ethnic origin, or any other distinguishing characteristics, is and must be treated as an end in himself or herself. To express this in the language of Sartre, human beings are not things that are meant to be used and abused or manipulated and enslaved. Every person, Kant believed, is endowed with a certain human dignity that renders him or her unique and inviolable. The moral law, therefore, compels us to recognize this dignity in others and in ourselves and imposes upon us the duty to act accordingly. This recognition does justice to the most fundamental characteristic of every human being, his or her absolute freedom as a moral agent, a freedom that we deny when we behave toward people as if they were objects. Surely, Kant understood that in most human relationships and in the ways in which people deal with one another, there is a natural tendency to convert people into objects. A friend, for instance, is often conceived of merely as someone who pleases us and whose services are available to us. Love, likewise, is sometimes understood in the same way. What does the phrase 'I love you' mean, if not 'You give me pleasure' or 'I like you'? When that pleasure is no longer rendered, love, too, disappears, because we cease to be interested in the *object* that we once 'loved'.

What is important to remember of Kant's ethical views is his insistence on separating moral values from natural characteristics and tendencies and his commitment to establish them on a rational foundation. Neither happiness nor feelings nor social norms nor what is interpreted as God's will nor, in fact, anything else can take the place of a rational commitment to act for the sake of duty alone, and this duty is given substance in the categorical imperative. As in the instance of other ethical theories, however, it is not difficult to detect weaknesses and discover problems in that of Kant. Still, it remains in the history of ethics one of the most ingenious and edifying efforts to introduce order into a field in which controversy and confusion have prevailed. Since the time of Socrates, the search for moral values has engaged the imagination of practically every philosopher, and the results, as the examples adduced in this chapter show, have been varied and inconclusive. Whether in ethical relativism, in ethical naturalism, in ethical absolutism (of which Kant's approach is an example), or in any other attempt to make sense of those moral words that every child learns early in his life, we find perplexities and areas of profound disagreement. Still, somehow we cannot fail to recognize that, despite this fact, the structure of our selves, as Socrates insisted, is determined by the values that we uphold and by the way in which those values guide our conduct. For this reason, ethics has remained at the core of the adventure of philosophy as its most urgent task. The last thing that we would like to do is to side with ethical nihilism and conclude that there is nothing to say about moral values because they are nothing. Without them, our lives, individually and collectively, would be irremediably meaningless.

# *The Problem of the Existence of God*

"The fool said in his heart, 'There is no God'" (Psalms 14:1, 53:1). With this severe admonition, the Bible gives expression to the common religious attitude with which those who deny the existence of God are viewed. In the same passage, we are told that the fool is corrupt, that his actions are abominable, and that there is nothing good in him. His rejection of God is, therefore, not merely a manifestation of foolishness and ignorance but a sign of his evil character. Neither in mind nor in will is the atheist a person worthy of praise. There was in the fourth century B.C. a Greek philosopher named Theodorus of Cyrene from whom we hear precisely the opposite of the biblical statement: the belief in God or gods is found only among mindless fools in whose minds and lives one comes upon every sort of vice and wickedness.

With these two discordant notes, we can begin these reflections on the problem of the existence of God. As the two extremes in a wide spectrum of views and convictions, the biblical statement on the one hand and, on the other, Theodorus the Atheist (as he became known) present to us two irreconcilable positions. In the former, God appears as an undeniable reality that only fools dare to reject, and in the latter, God is deemed to be an illusion that only fools insist on accepting. Between these two extremes, we find all sorts of possibilities and a great variety of approaches, many of which have been examined and defended by philosophers. In the adventure of philosophy, it would be surprising not to come upon this circumstance. For it is undeniable that the belief in God or gods has played an important part in all cultures at all times, and thus, as an important component of human experience, philosophers have been compelled to come to grips with it, sometimes in order to make sense of its presence among people, especially as the basis of religion, and sometimes in order to account for its presence or absence in themselves. Today, centuries after the Bible was written and after Theodorus lived, the controversy about the existence of God remains as intense as in ancient times. Occasionally, new ideas have emerged among philosophers, but these have generally proved to be renditions and restatements of what we find among our classical ancestors.

The apparent futility of arguing about the problem of the existence of God has not deterred philosophers from undertaking repeatedly the task of shedding light on it. This is perfectly understandable for two reasons. First, it is unquestionable that the belief in God, or in some superior power that is responsible for the existence of the world and that oversees its processes, is found among many people. As such, then, it is a persistent reality of human experience, and if philosophy is committed to the task of making sense of the world, it cannot ignore it. The question of the existence of God may be one of those that Kant viewed as unanswerable at least from the point of view of reason, but it is also one of those that he regarded as unavoidable. Second, in considering this question, hosts of issues arise in practically all areas of philosophical interest, and a review of it, regardless of assumptions and conclusions, brings to the surface a whole world of valuable ideas. For these reasons, we cannot avoid dealing with it, difficult and treacherous as this undertaking may be.

The concept of God (or gods) is intimately intertwined with the acceptance of a religion, and this makes the task of discussing it from a rational and detached point of view exceedingly difficult. The emotional ties with which religions bind their adherents occasionally incapacitate them for critical reflection about the concept that underlies their faith. Talking about God and, even worse, subjecting to rational examination the belief in God are generally not welcomed endeavors, for it is feared that in the light of reason, beliefs may become unsteady and that even a loss of faith may occur. This may or may not be so. Still, if we embark on philosophical explorations, questions such as "Does God exist?" "What basis is there to believe in God?" "What does the concept of God mean?" "How can we believe in an almighty and benevolent God in a world in which there is so much suffering?" "How can human beings have free will if God already knows the future?" and other similar questions must be raised. Some maintain that both questions and answers concerning God presuppose faith in God if they are to be meaningful. Otherwise, they argue, nothing can be accomplished. Generally, however, the path outlined by philosophy is different. It is not "faith seeking understanding," to use a phrase of Saint Anselm of Canterbury, but reason seeking to understand what those who possess the gift of faith believe about God.

In our effort to make sense of the problem of the existence of God, our first task should be to clarify the meaning of the word 'God', but here an avalanche of difficulties comes to us from all directions. This word means different things, and its meanings are deeply embedded in historical and cultural contexts. Let us set aside polytheism and anthropomorphism, the examination of which may not be fruitful in this discussion. In polytheism, as exemplified in the beliefs of the ancient Greeks and Romans and of other cultures of the past, God is not conceived of either as one or as transcendent, but as several or many and as physical in some sense. The Greeks believed in gods, lots of them, similar to human beings in some respects, powerful yet limited, immortal yet not eternal, knowledgeable yet not all-knowing, magnificent yet imperfect. Invariably, they were viewed as part of the *physis* of the universe and as subject to change and to the processes that govern the world. They existed *in* the world, not beyond the world, and were generally conceived of in the shape of human beings, for which reason we refer to them as anthropomorphic (from two Greek words, *anthropos* and *morphe*, that is, 'man' and 'shape'). Some were male while others were female; some were beautiful and others ugly; some were good and just and others bad and unjust.

Although polytheism is an important idea that deserves careful study in anthropology and in history, it is only a subject of marginal interest in philosophical discussions. The conception of God that underlies monotheism, in which God appears as one and transcendent, is, however, a subject with which philosophical analysis must cope. Historically, this conception is not as ancient as some religious creeds would like their adherents to believe. It emerged in the course of time out of polytheism and other ancient beliefs such as animism. Its earliest manifestations among the Jews are traceable to the time of the prophet Jeremiah (seventh century B.C.), in whose description of God as "the fountain of living waters" (Jeremiah 2:14) we discern the outlines of the God that would become the basis of Judaism and Christianity. Among the Greeks, the oldest expression of monotheism comes from the fragments of Xenophanes, a Presocratic philosopher of the early fifth century B.C. With him, the anthropomorphic gods begin to recede into the background in order to make room for a God who is not like human beings or like any other thing, who exists in a dimension beyond time and space, and who is one and only one. If we insist on looking for a similar idea before the time of Jeremiah or Xenophanes, we will probably be disappointed.

What, then, is this God of monotheism? Before we venture into a discussion about his existence, we must have some idea about him,[1] because how can we talk about his existence if we have no information about him and if no distinctive characteristics can serve as the basis for a definition? The problem is, however, that in attempting to *define* the concept of God, we come upon obstacles that may be impossible to overcome. To define means to set a limit. When we define, for

---

1. I have followed with some hesitation the convention of using masculine pronouns in referring to God. This convention may be a vestige of the anthropomorphism of ancient religions.

instance, the concept 'dog', we could say that it refers to a four-legged animal that barks. 'Four-legged', 'animal', and 'barking' are the attributes that distinguish a dog from other things. A table is not a dog because it is neither an animal nor does it bark, despite its having four legs. A cat is not a dog because it does not bark, even though it is a four-legged animal. Each attribute in a definition sets the thing apart from other things, and the greater the number of attributes, the more specific and clear the definition is. In the case of the concept of God, however, what limits can we set for it and what attributes can we assign to it? If God is eternal and infinite, neither temporal nor spatial attributes can belong to him, and if he is immaterial, no physical characteristics can distinguish him. An immaterial, eternal, and infinite being cannot, therefore, be *defined*. For this reason, some theologians have argued that there is *nothing* that can be *said* about God and have opted for what is called a *via negativa*, a negative approach. Is God a stone? No. Is God a cloud? No. Is God a star? No. Is God a body? No. Is God a soul? No. Is God old? No. Is God young? No. Who or what, then, is God? God is neither this nor that nor any other thing. But if this is so, our only option is silence, because nothing can be *said* about him. Our understanding of concepts and ideas, and our perception of things, proceed on the basis of limits and distinctions, and human language is meaningful only when we can express ourselves in terms of specifications. Imagine, for instance, that someone were to say that he met someone who was very tall. How tall, we could ask, to which he might reply that as tall as the distance between the earth and the moon. Surely, we would not believe him, but we could still make some sense of his answer: the person was thousands of miles in height. If, however, he were to tell us that the person was so tall that he had no limit in height, we would be baffled. His answer would be meaningless, because we could neither visualize nor conceptualize his experience.

Yet, when someone speaks about God, are we not in a similar situation? According to Wittgenstein, we should remain silent concerning matters about which there is nothing to say. Should we, then, following the *via negativa*, keep absolute silence about God? Gregory of Nyssa, an early medieval theologian, spoke of God as a great cloud of darkness, inside of which no human eye can penetrate, which explains the enormous feeling of despair that overcomes the soul in its search for God. Only, perhaps, in the highest state of mystical rapture, attainable by very few, can the divine reality be revealed in a rough and indistinct outline. Concerning God, nothing can be known by perception or by reason, and, as Clement of Alexandria insisted, we are condemned to know *that* God exists while remaining in silence and in ignorance about *what* or *who* he is. Yet, how is it possible to affirm the existence of something without having even the slightest notion as to what it is whose existence we affirm?

Silence about God, however, is rare among people. Few words are as common and as often used as the word 'God'. People talk and preach about God, pray aloud to God, argue about God and sometimes even kill one another in the name of God, and use his name in all sorts of contexts. When in pain or when in the presence of something unexpected, do we not exclaim "Oh my God!" as if this phrase were an inborn linguistic reflex? When we swear to tell the truth, do we not add "So help me God"? When criminals are executed, are they not dispatched with the words "May God have mercy on your soul"? Even in some countries, every piece of currency bears the name of God, and people affirm that they belong to "one nation under God." All this is perplexing, if, indeed, there is nothing that can be said about God. Still, we can make some sense of this situation by examining various ideas concerning the relationship between faith and reason.

In the history of philosophy, especially in medieval and modern times, two disparate views have been held concerning the relationship between faith and reason, both of which are accompanied with an assortment of implications for the problem of the existence of God. There is on one side the conviction that faith and reason are irreconcilable and mutually exclusive. On the other side, we come upon two alternatives: either through reason we are able to strengthen and clarify our faith, or reason can guide us in the direction of faith. The conviction that faith and reason are irreconcilable takes us to fideism, agnosticism, or atheism, while in the idea that faith can be supported by reason, we encounter various views that are classed together under the name of theism. In fideism, faith is seen as the only avenue that leads to the belief in God, and reason is regarded as an impertinent distraction that may hinder us in our commitment to faith or as an obstacle that can undermine that commitment.[2] In some instances of fideism, reason—the capacity to examine matters critically—is rejected. Occasionally, we hear from the advocates of fideism that the source of reason is the Devil himself and that when we fall into the temptation of *thinking* about the world or about ourselves, we manifest the wickedness of our depraved nature. After all, the fruit that brought about the fall of Adam and Eve (through whose sin we are all born sinners) came from the Tree of Knowledge—"the desirable tree that promises to make us wise" (Genesis 3:6). If the progenitors of the human race had kept their curiosity in check, they might not have developed their ability to reason, but they would have preserved their simple faith and their innocence.

From this fideistic point of view, the adventure of philosophy must be seen as a journey that can only take us to unbelief and evil. Thus, for instance, Saint Jerome (second century A.D.) denounced the pretensions of philosophers and

---

2. The term 'fideism' is derived from the Latin word for 'faith' (*fides*). Although formally condemned in 1834 by Pope Gregory XVI, fideism has remained, both in Christianity and in other religions, a persistent and widespread conviction and attitude.

condemned their misguided efforts to understand rationally the mystery of reality. According to him, reason leads to doubt and even to the abandonment of faith, and so, for those fortunate souls who have the gift of faith, what advantage could there be in enlisting the aid of reason? Tertullian, an early Christian apologist, left for us a phrase that sums up the essence of fideism: "*Credo quia absurdum est*," which means "I believe because it is absurd." The Latin word *quia* ('because') is the key term in this phrase. It is not that we should believe *despite* the absurdity of faith. We must believe precisely *because* what we believe is absurd. Indeed, the more absurd our faith may be, the more eager we should be to embrace it.

From the point of view of reason, the belief that the world was created by an eternal, benevolent, and omnipotent God, who chose to redeem humanity through the death and resurrection of his only son—this strange belief, argued Tertullian, is unquestionably a scandal, an absurdity, a manifestation of madness in the eyes of those who appeal to reason in order to make sense of the world. No wonder that when Saint Paul spoke before the Athenians about the resurrection of the dead at the end of time, some laughed at him and shook their heads in disbelief (Acts 17:32). What else could they have done, accustomed as they were to hear philosophers talk rationally about the world? But precisely because faith is a scandal and an absurdity, we should adhere to it. This is the essence of fideism. The distrust and the uneasiness with which religious people occasionally view philosophy are rooted in the conviction that faith and reason are irreconcilable and that, if a choice has to be made, faith, not reason, must be chosen. Knowledge about God does not come from thinking about him, but through the illumination made possible by a leap of faith in which reason is set aside and faith is accepted. This attitude is at the basis of the adherence to religion that is found among many people. Saint Thérèse of Lisieux made it plain when she insisted that instead of talking *about* God, we must devote ourselves to talking *to* God through prayer.

If, however, faith and reason are irreconcilable, there is the option of choosing the latter, and this is what some philosophers and scientists have done, resulting in either a rejection of the idea of God or a suspension of judgment. The former of these results is atheism, while the latter is agnosticism. The word 'agnostic' is Greek in origin and means literally 'no knowledge'. Thus, the agnostic argues that there is no evidence that can possibly convince us that God exists. Charles Darwin, to whom we owe the modern theory of evolution, concluded that nothing in the world of nature points to an intelligent creator, a cosmic organizer, who could have been responsible for the processes of the natural world. The order and the purpose that we discover in the world are not facts of the world but merely projections of our own ideas through which we explain our experiences. In itself, the world has neither order nor purpose. Furthermore, as others have argued, if God is understood as infinite and eternal, how can we make sense of him if our own capacity to reason is bound by the limits of space and time? Earlier, we commented on the problem of defining God and saw how every definition imposes a limit, a boundary. If, however, the idea of God admits of neither limits nor boundaries, how can we construct a definition of him? Agnosticism, while not denying the possibility of his existence perhaps on a plane unknown to us and beyond our capacity to think, turns its glance away from such a possibility and declares that nothing fruitful can be said or known about God from a rational point of view.

Although the line that separates agnosticism from atheism is often blurry and in ordinary speech these terms are used interchangeably, we should recognize a distinction between them. Whereas agnosticism finds all evidence concerning God inconclusive and may have difficulty even understanding what the word 'God' means, atheism denies that God exists, and does not hesitate to adduce reasons why his existence should be rejected. Examples of atheism in philosophy and science are not difficult to find. From Theodorus of Cyrene among the Greeks to Nietzsche, Freud, and Sartre in modern times, there is a long list of thinkers who have argued that the basis on which religions are generally established, that is God, is groundless. Their arguments are many and varied and are supported by anthropological and psychological explanations of the belief in God, as well as by considerations concerning the nature of religious knowledge. Monotheism, they remind us, grew out of the polytheism and animism of primitive and ancient cultures, in which ignorance about natural processes led people to explain them in anthropomorphic ways. Fantasy and myth, superstition and magic—the basis of explanation of the primitive mind—together with the inability of people to control nature and with their natural fear of death, gave birth to gods, demons, and ghosts, and from these the God of monotheism eventually emerged. But he, too, is as fictional and mythical as his ancestors. When, as Critias, a Sophist of Socrates' time, maintained, the ruling classes need to keep the masses under subjection, the fiction of God or gods is their most effective tool. A sophisticated mind, however, sees through these deceptions and illusions and recognizes that man is alone in the universe and must forge his own future without appealing to an illusory and nonexisting father-image in heaven. God, or rather the concept of God, as Nietzsche proclaimed, is dead, for his usefulness as a means to explain the world and as a source of moral values is only a historical curiosity.

There is also the so-called argument from evil, which we find repeatedly among the adherents of atheism. Already stated in classical times by the Roman philosopher Lucretius, this argument has been rephrased in countless ways in modern times. The common monotheistic conception of God depicts him as omnipotent, omniscient, and benevolent. In these attributes, we find something that approaches a definition of him. His omnipotence is such that nothing is beyond his control. Neither the laws of nature nor the destinies of human beings are beyond his power, and when he intervenes in the world, miracles occur. Unlike Zeus and the other gods of polytheism, whose power was limited, God has no limitations, for he is almighty. His omniscience allows him to know all things, and past, present, and future are known to him. True wisdom belongs only to him. His benevolence makes him supremely good, and nothing but the well-being of his creatures, especially those created in his image, can ever be in his loving mind. How wonderful to have a parent endowed with omnipotence, omniscience, and benevolence, for under his protection we are free from suffering and concerns!

Yet, what do we see all around us other than suffering and pain, abandonment, and misery, precisely among those of God's creatures for whom he supposedly created the heavens and the earth? Evil, understood in the sense of suffering and pain, permeates every human life, sometimes more, sometimes less, irrespective of how good or bad people are. It comes from nature, as in catastrophes, earthquakes, plagues, sickness, old age, and innumerable other ways. Often, too, it comes from people's actions, from their mistakes and selfishness, from their evil will, and from their barbarities and atrocities through which they cause untold pain and misery to others. Viewed from this pessimistic yet somehow realistic perspective, human life turns out to be an absurdity, as if we had been created by God only to be abandoned as unwanted children. Evil, then, is a condition that seems to be endemic in the universe—at least in that minuscule part of the universe that we know. But if this is so, or appears to be so, what sense are we to make of its creator and overseer, an omnipotent, omniscient, and benevolent God? If experience shows that every human life is, as Schopenhauer observed, a comedy in its details but always a tragedy in the end, what shall we say about the existence of God and what role shall we assign to him in the world? How can we justify evil in a world created by God? Can we confidently say, as Socrates did at his trial, that if there is anything that can be affirmed with certainty, it is that nothing evil ever happens to a good person, when we know, or seem to know, that evils do happen to people who are blameless? When children suffer, how shall we justify their suffering?

Answers to these and similar questions abound. We can simply deny the existence of God. The reality of evil alone is sufficient for us to bracket away the belief in God, for it is absurd to imagine that a provident and loving God, whose power and knowledge are limitless, could allow for pain and suffering to engulf the human condition. For this to be possible, we would have to deny either that God is benevolent or that he is omniscient or that he is omnipotent, in which case he would no longer be the God to whom people of faith give their allegiance. He may be a 'lesser' god, like the anthropomorphic gods of ancient times, limited and constrained and tragically unable to set aright a creation gone bad, but then his usefulness and efficacy as creator and overseer of the world would dissipate into thin air. For this and other reasons, the atheist rejects as an illusion the belief in his existence. We have come into the world as the result of natural processes over which we have no control and will pass away in the endless collection of cycles and transformations of a universe that has no ground and no explanation. In the brief time that is allotted to each one of us between birth and death, all we can do is to manage as best as we can, with the certainty that nothing above and beyond us can render any assistance. This realization entails courage and resignation, but, short of intellectual dishonesty, can we choose anything else?

An alternative to atheism is provided by deism, a view in which a curious solution is proposed for the problem of evil but in which the ordinary conception of God undergoes a radical transformation. On November 1, 1755, on a religious holiday and precisely at noon, a terrible earthquake devastated the city of Lisbon in Portugal, causing indescribable destruction and suffering, killing thousands of people, many of whom were attending religious services. On that occasion, Voltaire, a French philosopher known for his critical stance toward organized religion, wrote his "Poem Upon the Lisbon Disaster," in which he asks about the whereabouts of God when the earthquake occurred. Was he absent or unaware of the circumstances, or was he unable to lend his assistance? Could he not have prevented the catastrophe? Was he unconcerned about the plight of his creatures? In other words, why, if God is real, could so hideous a tragedy have taken place? The famous Lisbon earthquake, despite being one of the biggest earthquakes on record, is not a unique event, and neither is Voltaire's reaction. We all have found ourselves in situations when, because of some tragedy or some unfortunate circumstance, we experience a sense of perplexity about the presence of God in the world.

For some, such situations are bearable because of their faith and their ability to transform what manifests itself at first as a great evil into an event that, as part of God's design, is not an evil. For others, the result may be a loss of faith, for nothing, they may argue, can explain away senseless and indiscriminate pain and suffering. Still for others, as in the case of Voltaire, there is nothing perplexing about an earthquake that wrecks countless lives and leaves behind a long trail of misery. The questions raised in his poem were rhetorical, not to say sarcastic, because he knew the answer. It is not that God does not exist, for he does exist, but (and this is the essence of deism) not as an active presence in the world. God created the world and set it aright at the beginning of time and henceforth terminated his relationship with it. Like a clockmaker, who finishes his clock and sets it at the right time and walks away from it, so, too, God made the world and established for it inflexible natural laws and removed himself from it. In deism, then, there is no divine providence in whatever happens in the world, and earthquakes and other catastrophes occur or do not occur irrespective of how they may affect God's favorite creatures—human beings. In the absence of God's intervention, what need could there be for prayers and rituals, for hymns of praise and thanksgiving, and for all the practices of religions? It makes no sense either to praise God for those aspects and circumstances of nature that are beneficial to us or to blame him for those that cause pain and suffering. Neither in the former nor in the latter does God play any role.

The concept of God that surfaces in deism, however, has left many people, including philosophers, unimpressed. It is true that it manages to solve the problem of evil by absolving God of any responsibility in the matter, but it is also true that it proposes a thin and skeletal conception of God that not even the most intransigent among atheists would care to disprove and that theists and believers would find useless. For God to be a significant reality in human life it is necessary to conceive of him as present and active in the affairs of the world, precisely as portrayed in the Bible, a reading of which may leave us with the impression that God has little else to do but to be concerned with what human beings do and with how they fare, almost as if he needed them as much as they need him. In fideism and in theism, benevolence and omnipotence are invariably attributed to him. His loving and almighty presence in the world is our assurance that we are under his protection. This conviction, however, brings us back to the problem of evil. If God is benevolent and omnipotent, why was Lisbon reduced to ruins and his believers crushed under the collapsing roofs of churches? *That* is what Voltaire wanted to know. His poem on the earthquake was publicly burned in Paris, and it is not difficult to imagine what the responses of people of faith could have been.

The advocates of fideism and theism have ways of dealing with the problem of evil in order to invalidate or at least weaken the argument from evil. Their responses to the questions posed by Voltaire merit consideration, because, if nothing else, they bring to the surface important philosophical issues. It is argued, for instance, that the identification of evil with pain and suffering is faulty. Is it not possible that even the worst catastrophes may yield positive results not only for the victims but for humanity in general? Is it not a fact that even out of the most devastating tragedy some good may come? Suffering has redeeming qualities for the sufferer and for those who witness his suffering. Moreover, we learn to become better persons and to strengthen our characters through difficulties and vicissitudes, and societies grow in abundance and vigor precisely through the process of renewal that the accidents of nature (sometimes called 'acts of God') inflict upon them. The modern city of Lisbon grew out of the wreckage of 1755, more vigorous, more affluent, more full of life. Besides, how else could we appreciate our blessings except by experiencing ill fortune? For the good to have meaning, it is necessary to experience the bad, just as light is best appreciated when seen against the background of darkness. Furthermore, our knowledge of the world is limited, and neither reason nor sense experience reveals anything but an insignificant part of reality. In God's grand scheme for his creation, a human life is as inconsequential as that of an ant that is crushed under our feet. How, then, is it possible for us to pass judgment on the plan of creation, knowing so little and being so limited? A child may conclude that his parents are cruel and heartless when they punish him or force him to undergo pain to secure his health. *They*, not *he*, however, know the purpose of the 'evil' that they make him suffer, which, far from being an evil, is only a painful means to his greater good. His ignorance leads him to misinterpret their actions, which are evil in his eyes but that, in reality, are not. It is likewise in the case of human beings who misunderstand the meaning of natural occurrences and fail to make sense of their role in God's design.

This design, according to theism, includes a reality that explains pain and suffering. God, at least from some religious points of view, guarantees that the destiny of every human life is not confined to the physical world. The body, a material thing that disintegrates after death, is only a part of every person, the other part, far more important, being the soul, where consciousness and personal identity reside. This soul, akin to God in its immateriality, does not perish with the death of the body but remains alive and proceeds then to its final destination, either to unending bliss in the presence of God or to eternal damnation. Its fate is determined by the character and content of its life while in this world, and pain and suffering, if humbly accepted, have a cleansing effect on it. Eternal salvation is earned not only by obeying God's commands but also by spiritually profiting from the unhappy moments that flow from the natural world and from the actions of others. But if this marvelous tale is true, who in his right mind would not welcome every opportunity to suffer every disease, every pain, if the reward is so great? Should we not emulate the example of Christian monks, who through mortification seek to tame the natural and sinful impulses of the body, hoping thereby to gain eternal bliss? Their asceticism, that is, their war on pleasure, is a means to attain greater pleasure not in this world but in another. Surely, on *this* basis, the problem of evil has been solved. Faith has apparently supplied us with the answer.

Yet, there is another perplexity that needs to be addressed. As we have seen, not only is God conceived of as benevolent and omnipotent but also as omniscient and omnipresent, for he knows everything and is everywhere, as we read in the Bible (Psalms 11:4-5; John 1:18). Past and future are present in his mind, and he knows now what I will do in the future. All my actions are known to him, as if my entire life were a mere moment for him. How, then, is it possible for me to choose freely the course of my life if it is already known by God? Is it not reasonable to assume that his omniscience makes it impossible for my future actions to be undetermined and uncertain? Am I not like a character in a film that I have seen many times, and whose actions I know in advance because I have already seen them? My uncertainty about the future creates in me the illusion of indeterminacy, that is, the belief that my will is free, but in reality the 'film' of my life has already been made and has been seen by God. If even my future after death, whether salvation or damnation, is already known by God, then I must conclude that every moment of my life, every action of mine, and my final destiny are wholly predestined, not by the causes and effects that make up the universe or by my character and predispositions, as is affirmed in determinism, but by the presence of an omniscient God.

This belief in predestination has emerged from time to time in the history of ideas, but has often been rejected by the adherents of theism, even when they maintain that it is rationally impossible to explain human freedom against the background of the omniscience of God. How human beings can be free if God is omniscient is, according to Saint Augustine, a mystery. Still, we must affirm both the existence of God and the reality of human freedom. But why must we accept two beliefs that are apparently mutually exclusive? From the point of view of theism, the former of them is not only an article of faith but is, as Saint Thomas Aquinas insisted, a belief supported by rational arguments. The belief in the freedom of the will, moreover, allows us to make at least some sense of the reality of evil in human life. Earthquakes and other catastrophes are natural events that, if we grant the presence of God in the world, may be interpreted as manifestations of his design. But pain and suffering also come in great abundance from what people do to people. One only has to bring to mind the wars of extermination that have taken place so often, where in a methodic and systematic way evil has been inflicted on innumerable people. How are we to account for such happenings, especially when the victims are children and when no redeeming signs are forthcoming? There, too, we could ask questions reminiscent of those asked by Voltaire. Is God unable or unwilling to protect those who suffer at the hands of torturers and abusers? How could humanly created evil be a part of his design?

The answer of theism is that in creating human beings, God gave them a free will to choose between good and evil and that when the latter is chosen, it is not God from whom it comes but from the wickedness of human beings. We have gone astray from the beginning and our ways are contrary to what God intended for us to be. He left for us the responsibility of choosing what is good, but we have seldom heeded his voice. Freedom, then, provides an answer for at least the evil that comes from people's actions.

Still, despite the assurance with which theism and, even more, fideism dismiss the problem of evil, questions remain, but these, too, are answerable if a certain faith is accepted. Of course, if we believe that this life is only a temporary stage through which we must pass, a testing ground as it were, from which we are to move onto a different and more real dimension, then evil dissipates as if it were only a disturbing nightmare of no consequence for those who expect salvation. As for the others, the perpetrators of evil, they will find their just reward in the flames of eternal damnation, where their sufferings will more than balance out the sufferings and pains for which they were responsible in this life.

In the Bible (Luke 16:20-31), there is a story in which we hear of a certain beggar named Lazarus, a man full of sores, who lived at the gates of the house of some opulent and arrogant glutton. For years, and hardly able to survive, Lazarus begged for assistance from the rich man, and was always rejected. Eventually, both men died. Lazarus "was carried by the angels into Abraham's bosom," while the rich man was plunged into hell, from where, seeing Lazarus enjoying eternal bliss, he would cry out, saying "Father Abraham, have mercy on me, and send Lazarus, that he may dip the tip of his finger in water, and cool my tongue; for I am tormented in this flame." Unmoved by the man's suffering, Abraham replied, "Son, remember that in your life you received good things, and Lazarus had only evil things. Now he is comforted and you are tormented."

This parable unveils for us a perfect solution for the reality of evil, the evil that nature and fate inflict upon us and the evil that people choose. Undeserved evil is amply compensated with everlasting happiness and wilfully chosen evil, with eternal damnation. The poor, the oppressed, the persecuted, the sick, and all those who suffer in this life will be rewarded with joys that will obliterate the memories of their sufferings, while the wicked, the oppressors, the rich, and all those who are responsible for increasing the burden of human suffering will be punished in hell for all eternity. Who could then say that God's justice is not real? Theism and fideism come out triumphant from their confrontation with evil, and Voltaire's questions are convincingly answered. Reward and punishment in another life provide a formidable solution for the problem of evil, a problem that has consistently remained a powerful argument *against* the existence of God. His benevolence and his providence emerge unscathed, and even his omnipotence is not irreparably challenged, except that we could argue that a being who is truly almighty could have developed for his creatures a simpler way to gain eternal bliss. Why is suffering on earth necessary to deserve being in his presence? Still, the problem of evil stands apparently solved.

Yet, is this truly so, or have we injected into our solution an element that from the point of view of reason is extraneous and illicit? Have we not argued against an argument against the existence of God precisely by reaffirming the reality of him whose existence is in question? If so, we are guilty of a *petitio principii*, a begging of the question. We began with the statement that if evil is real, God does not exist, and we countered with the statement that because God exists, evil is not as real as we may have initially thought. Moreover, in order to account for the evil that in the form of pain and suffering afflicts humanity, we insisted on the immortality of the soul, on the reality of rewards and punishments after death, and on the freedom of the will that allows people to choose good and evil. We insisted on these articles of faith, because we were convinced that in their absence the presence of evil *and* the existence of God are two irreconcilable alternatives. Somehow, however, we have found ourselves caught in circular reasoning, because in order to neutralize the argument from evil, we have affirmed precisely that which this argument seeks to invalidate, and we have introduced into our reasoning still other assertions, principally the immortality of the soul in the absence of which the problem of evil would remain unsolved. In order to make sense of the existence of God against the background of what is perceived as evil, we have to presuppose that the death of the body is not the end of the person, for the reality of God guarantees the immortality of the soul. Otherwise, how would compensation for pain and suffering be possible? The belief in a God who does not assure the continuation of life after death fails to satisfy our need to make sense of evil in human life, for which reason God and the immortality of the soul are twin ideas that are difficult to separate. The question is, however, whether such ideas can sustain the test of reason or whether, as in fideism, we may have to accept them despite their absurdity or even *because* of their absurdity.

What we find in theism is the conviction that even though faith is the primary avenue that leads to a belief in God, reason provides a secondary path that renders our faith reasonable. Thus, various arguments have sprung from theism in which what Locke called demonstrative knowledge of God is allegedly attained. The value of such arguments is, of course, a matter of controversy, and each one of their premises can be challenged. Often, we hear that they are not valid logical arguments but mere rationalizations of a conclusion that is at the outset taken for granted. If faith is not already present, they prove to be ineffective at least from the point of view of some philosophers. Still, the fool, let us remember, is the only one who would dare question or reject that which every sensible person affirms without hesitation. What makes, however, the belief in the existence of God a sensible belief? What arguments can be constructed that could possibly convince us that in adhering to faith we are not abdicating our capacity to reason? What line of reasoning can we follow to support the doctrine that "one true God and Lord can be known with certainty by the natural light of human reason," a doctrine affirmed by the Church? We will examine briefly several such arguments, some of which go back to medieval times and which have been rephrased and dissected countless times by modern philosophers.

There is, for instance, the argument from consensus, which has wide appeal among believers. In it, it is argued that the belief in God as the creator and overseer of the world is found in all societies and cultures and is somehow ingrained in practically all human beings. Even atheists and agnostics turn to God in moments of despair or when near death. There are, we are told, no atheists in the trenches, almost as if there were something within each human being that cries out for God's assistance when the world seems to be collapsing around us. Human consensus, therefore, points decisively in the direction of faith, and God emerges among us as a reality that cannot be challenged. Again, who but a fool could deny his existence? Critics of this argument, however, point out that while most people adhere to some belief in a divine presence in the world, this belief is by no means always the same as what one finds among theists, whose God is endowed with characteristics such as transcendence, omniscience, and benevolence.

This concept of God, central in religions such as Christianity and Judaism, is not found among the majority of human beings, either now or in the past. In religions such as Buddhism, Hinduism, and other Oriental religions, to which the majority of human beings belong, the idea of a monotheistic and transcendent God is foreign. In them, we come upon pantheism (the belief that God and the world are one) or upon all sorts of other beliefs, some of which are vestiges of the polytheistic and animistic religions of antiquity. In fact, in some of the most widespread religions, the case can be made that atheism lies at their basis. God, at least as he is conceived of in modern Western religions, plays no part in them. If, however, this is the case, we have to conclude that only a minority of human beings are inclined to accept the existence of God. If so, what consensus is there to support the belief in his existence? Furthermore, as noted earlier, monotheism is a late historical development that cannot be traced back before Xenophanes among the Greeks and Jeremiah among the Jews. Before them, gods and demons reigned supreme, and nature provided an ample source to convert all sorts of things (animals, trees, rivers, mountains, stars) into divine beings. Thus, neither contemporary statistical facts nor historical records support the thesis that most people have been or are attached to the belief in a monotheistic and transcendent God.

It can be argued, moreover, that the *need* to believe in a higher being is universal among people because of the misery and unhappiness in which they often live and, above all, because of their natural fear of death. Dying is a manifestation of the *physis* in which all things exist, and entropy is an unavoidable circumstance. Still, human beings have an incurable desire to remain in existence at all costs, and, aware as they are of the finality of life, what else can they do except to imagine a higher source of salvation from death, this source being, for many of them, God himself? Psychologically and sociologically and, we may even add, biologically, the *need* to believe in God is understandable and common among people, but wishful thinking does not create reality. We may all be waiting for the arrival of Godot, but Godot may not even exist.[3] Besides, arguing from a more philosophical

---

3. Godot is the main, albeit unseen, character in Samuel Beckett's play *Waiting for Godot*. The characters on the stage wait for him and yearn for his presence throughout this play, but in the end, of course, he never comes.

point of view, even if it could be shown that most people believe in God—the God of monotheism—*this* fact should leave us unmoved. The opinions of the many, as Socrates maintained, are seldom worthy of consideration and can easily misguide us, because they are often the result of unclear impressions and are generally based on uncritically accepted premises. If, as Diogenes believed, most people are either mad or nearly mad, why should we take into account what they say or think? Should we not rather imitate the practice of Phocion and cast our vote always against the majority and dismiss as senseless what most people find sensible?

A second argument for the existence of God, the moral argument, deserves more attention. It appears, for instance, in the writings of Kant and, as in the cases of other arguments, it has been formulated in various ways. It is often expressed in terms of a hypothetical argument: If God does not exist, human life has no purpose. Human life, however, must have a purpose. Therefore, God exists. In another formulation, we are told that unless God exists, moral values, which render human life meaningful, have no basis and that since it is necessary for moral values to have a basis, we must affirm the reality of God.

As we saw in the previous chapter, it may be true that God is for many people the basis of their morality, for without a benevolent God, human existence would turn out to be a collection of meaningless moments of no significance. We are born to die and to undergo between birth and death a series of truncated experiences that lead nowhere and mean nothing at all. Could it be, as Kierkegaard once asked, that we are nothing but biological tubes for eating, excreting, and reproducing? Are we condemned by the randomness of evolution to hope for what is beyond hope and to imagine ourselves to be what we are not? Could we be, like ants and worms, only the accidental products of a nature that has neither an origin nor a purpose? Is that what human existence is? Where do all our efforts lead except to an eternity of unconsciousness in which we become extinct? Could human life be meaningless in the sense that, in the end, it amounts to nothing?

Three answers can be given to these disturbing questions. We could say, in agreement with Kierkegaard, that the meaninglessness of human existence is only an illusion and that the bleakness of the world is merely the result of our inability to 'see' what lies beyond us. But what could lie beyond us and what could dissipate the apparent senselessness of our lives if not God, who is conceived of as the source of our being and our ultimate purpose? Indeed, if God did not exist, not only human life but everything else would be a futile and pointless manifestation of the *physis* that constitutes the universe, which would reveal itself as an absurdity without limits and without direction. But since *that* cannot be the case, what alternative have we but to take a daring leap of faith and affirm the existence of the only ground on which a moral purpose can be planted? As a postulate of reason that ensures our moral meaningfulness, to use Kant's language, God must be accepted as an unquestionable reality. We may never know *what* God is, for that knowledge transcends the limits of reason, but we know *that* God is, for that knowledge is indispensable if human life is to have a moral foundation.

A different answer, however, is possible. If God does not exist, human life has no meaning. Well—God does not exist, therefore human life has no meaning and there is nothing more to say about it. This answer, which, for lack of a better expression, we can call the philosophy of the absurd, is not as uncommon as we may think. Thoreau once said that most people live lives of quiet desperation. It may be truer to say that some people recognize the futility of all their endeavors and activities and are aware of the abyss of nothingness from which they came and into which they will return, while others, the majority, live life as if on an endless holiday, like children in an amusement park, drowning in diversions and projects the existential emptiness in which they live. The difference between them is that whereas the latter are lucky to have only a spark of self-awareness and live as if in a dream, the former are cursed by nature with a clear mind that forces them to recognize the absurdity of existence. In them, a nihilistic response colors every aspect of their lives. This response, eloquently expressed in writings associated with existentialism, sees the world for what it is, namely, an unexplainable chain of causes and effects leading nowhere and human life as a transitory collection of frustrated and frustrating endeavors to find meaning where there is none. In a somber mood of pessimistic nihilism, Diogenes once said that if the human species were to disappear, there should be as much cause of regret as if bees and wasps became extinct, and if this is true of the species as a whole, what would we say about the value of one individual life? Like all other creatures in nature, we are bound to fail in whatever we do, because the end is always the same—nothingness. Even the most serious concerns and the most inspiring undertakings are ultimately only games and fleeting pastimes of no consequence. Why, then, should we even bother with the question of the existence of God?

There is yet another answer. It denies the main premise of the moral argument—if God does not exist, human life has no meaning—but insists that despite the fact that God does not exist, human life can still be invested with meaning. Since God is dead, to use Nietzsche's phrase, it is we who have to create meaning for our individual lives. It may not be a transcendent meaning and its purpose may not be the attaining of happiness in another world, for how could that be so if God does not exist? The problem is, however, how to create or invent meaning in a world that has none. Various solutions have been proposed by philosophers in which we encounter repeatedly the same theme: live each moment of your life as if it were the last moment, or, in a language reminiscent of Kant's categorical imperative, act as if your actions were absolutely meaningful or as if the entire human species depended on them. For this, however, a commitment to reason is necessary, for, otherwise, how could we construct out of the sequence of our actions an edifice that, when death arrives, we could judge it to have been worthy of our efforts? In Stoicism and Epicureanism and even in classical Cynicism, the emphasis lies on the structuring of life in a rational way, forgetful of the reality or lack of reality of a God that may be, after all, only the product of wishful thinking. Ours, not God's, is the responsibility of investing our individual lives with meaning through our choices.

The fundamental issue that lies at the heart of the moral argument is that its strength seems to depend on the prior acceptance of the existence of God, an acceptance that is not the fruit of reasoning but the result of faith. Hence, for those who have faith, the argument lends support to the idea of God as the basis of meaningfulness, but for those who lack that faith, the argument may be only a linguistic game of little value. Something similar can be said in the context of other theistic arguments, as in the case of the teleological argument or argument from design. The name of this argument is derived from the Greek word *telos*, which has a variety of meanings such as 'purpose', 'goal', and 'design'. Already found in medieval writings, as in those of Saint Thomas Aquinas, the teleological argument reappears in various philosophical and literary contexts with surprising stubbornness. Different versions of this argument can be found among philosophers and theologians, but in the end they all point in the same direction.

It was advanced in the eighteenth century by William Paley, who argued that if there is anything outside of faith that can convince us of God's existence it is the design or *telos* that permeates the universe. Let us imagine, for instance, that we find a watch in the middle of the desert—a watch telling the right time. What would be the most logical inference or sensible conclusion about our discovery? Could we argue, for example, that given enough time and through the agency of natural forces (winds, earth tremors, and so on), there is a statistical probability that, by recombining grains of sand and other things, a watch might be created? Or imagine that as astronauts explore the moon they come upon a building with doors, windows, and other such things. Would it make sense to attribute the existence of that building to the natural changes undergone by the moon during the almost five billion years since its formation? In *Gulliver's Travels*, Jonathan Swift ironically entertains the possibility that thousands of monkeys playing with letters engraved on movable wooden blocks can reproduce at least once all the works of Shakespeare—of course, if given sufficient time. But just think about the matter: a watch created by shifting sands, a building erected by lunar changes, and the works of Shakespeare rewritten by an army of monkeys! Does it not defy the imagination to suppose that such things could happen? If we were to come upon a watch in the middle of the desert, our natural reaction would be to say that someone left it there, and if a building were found on the moon, we would conclude that it was built by somebody, a human being or an alien, who had the intelligence and capacity to build it. And, of course, the greater the complexity of the building, the greater the intelligence of the builder, for a created object generally reflects the mind of its creator. The idea that complex and purposeful things emerge randomly and accidentally in the course of time is not an adequate hypothesis to explain their existence, because chance and randomness do not produce order and purpose. Nothing can exhibit order or design in the absence of an intelligent designer.

Now, if we inspect the world that surrounds us, what do we see? Do we not discover in it clear manifestations of the most complex arrangement? Do the planets move randomly around the sun, or do they not follow paths determined by the laws of celestial mechanics, which are themselves expressions of mathematical arrangements? On the earth, do we not discern everywhere signs of order and purpose? The human body is made up of innumerable parts—bones, muscles, tissues, and other things—all of which function precisely as they do in virtue of a purpose, a design, for which they were made. More complex in arrangement than a watch or a building, and more impressive than the works of Shakespeare, every organism, even the humblest cockroach, reveals a perfect architectonic design. But if so, how else can we explain this undeniable reality, except by affirming the existence of a cosmic organizer responsible for the structure of the universe and for the order and purpose of its components? Are we not justified in asserting that the greatness of the universe points to the greatness of its creator, whom we call God? Is it not unreasonable to confront order and design and yet deny a source of order and a designer?

The strength of the teleological argument rests on the reality of order and design in the world and on the irrationality of presupposing that such characteristics are attributable to chance and randomness. Since the time of the Presocratics, the universe, in the sense of *kosmos*, has been viewed as an organized structure governed by rational laws that exhibit order and design. The parts of the human body, for instance, appear to have been designed to maintain the organism alive, and their functions display a sense of purpose that is difficult to deny. Why do we have teeth, and specifically the kind of teeth we have, except for the purpose of chewing the foods that ensure the continuation of life? Is not the human eye an organ of the greatest complexity imaginable, and is not its purpose to allow us to see? And with respect to the ecological processes everywhere exhibited by nature, is there room to doubt that every creature and every environment interact in purposeful ways that promote the continuation of the species, as if nature itself were following a preconceived plan? The laws of physics, in accordance with which atoms behave and planets and stars move, reveal the order that permeates the world. How, then, could we not recognize in all these processes the invisible hand of a cosmic organizer, whose intelligence and foresight have made all these things possible? Would we not be imitating the biblical fool, who, despite all the evidence, rejects the existence of God?

On reflection, however, the matter proves to be more complex. It all depends on what the evidence is and on what weight we attach to the impressions of the senses. It is easier to conclude from a watch that a watchmaker exists or from a building that an architect must have designed it or from a literary work that a writer must have been its author than to assume from our experience of the world that an intelligent cosmic agent could have set all this universal machinery in motion. In the eighteenth century, David Hume, who assumed a skeptical, not to say agnostic, attitude toward religious faith, called attention to this circumstance. We are well acquainted with the process by which a watch is made and we know the *telos* or purpose that guides its construction. We discover order and design in a watch only because we know in advance its purpose or *telos*. It is doubtful whether in the absence of this knowledge we could recognize its order and design.

In the case of the world, however, neither the process of its alleged construction nor its purpose is known. Watches are made to tell time, but what purpose are cats and squirrels supposed to fulfill, or planets or stars or the universe at large? Furthermore, when we claim to discover order and design in nature, are we not merely projecting our ideas onto our experiences? By itself, nature may or may not be endowed with order and design. Not knowing whether or not it has a purpose, we will never come to a conclusion on this matter. Perhaps, when we seem to discover order and design in nature we are only foisting upon it such ideas, which are themselves nothing by imaginative combinations that we create out of our sense perceptions and our experiences with objects like watches and buildings. Hence, the order that some allege permeates the universe may turn out to be a projection of a mental mechanism used by the mind to make sense of things. In itself, the world may or may not be a manifestation of a divine design, and randomness—the randomness of Democritus' atomic universe—could lie at the basis of all events and things. This skeptical attitude, of course, does not disprove the existence of God, but it does undermine the attempt of those who appeal to the teleological argument to bolster their faith in God.

Another argument advanced by theism, also proposed by Saint Thomas Aquinas, is the cosmological argument. Here, too, various versions are found. In one of them, we are asked to reason along these lines: (1) it is undeniable that everything is the result of a sufficient cause; (2) the world, therefore, must be conceived of as a chain of causes and effects; (3) this chain can be understood either as having no beginning (hence, the world would be uncaused) or as having a beginning, that is, as having a cause; (4) if the world has no beginning and is, therefore, uncaused, the world would not exist, because nothing comes into existence without a cause; (5) the fact is, however, that the world does exist; (6)

hence, the world must have had a cause that explains its having come into existence; (7) this universal cause is what we call God. Here, then, we have a wonderful example of the demonstrative knowledge of which Locke spoke: from our empirical knowledge of the way things are, we reach a conclusion that, while not evident in sense experience, is supported by reason. From our perception of the cause-effect relationship in which things and events exist, we derive the conviction that God exists.

Here, too, however, we find ourselves caught in a web of difficulties. The assertion that everything in the world is the effect of a sufficient cause is a reasonable assumption supported by experience. Every chicken comes from an egg, and every egg comes from another chicken. Every person has parents, and these had parents who also had parents. Whatever we encounter and whatever happens can be traced back to prior conditions, which, had they not existed, would not have caused the things that we experience. If my parents had died in childhood, I would not be writing this book, and it is as simple as that. Only in the world of magic and fantasy things appear to come from nowhere, but there what happens is that we lack the knowledge to recognize the causes, which leads us to conclude that there are no causes. Unquestionably, then, the real world is a collection of causes and effects in which nothing exists without a sufficient ground for being what it is. Hume argued, however, that the cause-effect relationship that appears to link things and events is ultimately not a fact of the world but the projection of *our* idea of causality onto our experiences, an idea that helps us to understand the regularity of natural events.

Still, I know that without my parents' intervention I would have never been born and that without their own parents' intervention they would have not been born, and in that sense I am the product of a long chain of causes and effects that extends into the past. For how long? Well, as long as the history of the human species, that is, several million years. And what about before its beginning? We have to think of the existence of other creatures before that time, back to the primitive amoebae from which all organisms are said to come. But what about these? Are they not, too, the effects of earlier things and conditions, when the earth and the solar system came into being out of the nebular cloud that modern cosmology imagines as the origin of *our* world some five billion years ago?

We could regress even further to the time when the universe is believed to have come into existence. Two possibilities are open for us: either our regression is infinite in the sense of not having a beginning or it is conceived of as having had a beginning. The first hypothesis would leave us in the presence of something that never began—a hypothesis supported by some of the Presocratics who, like Democritus, maintained that the universe is eternal. Without a beginning, however, the universe stands as never having come into existence and as being, therefore, unexplainable and groundless, which, according to theism, makes no sense. Hence, we must opt for the second hypothesis and affirm that since the universe must be explainable, we must postulate a first cause for it, and this first cause is what we call God from whose creative power the universe arose from nothingness. First there was only God, and then there was God *and* the world.

Yet, various questions immediately suggest themselves to us. The assertion may be plausible that without a beginning in time, the universe turns out to be unexplainable. To the critical question of metaphysics "Why is there something rather than nothing?" the answer could very well be the suspension of judgment that Pyrrho advocated: there is nothing to say about it. It may be distressing to live in a world in which we can explain things and events that happen *within* the universe, that is, in time and space, but not the universe itself. Such may just be the unhappy reality that we must face. The universe may be eternal—timeless, without beginning and without end—and, at least for us who are accustomed to account for things in terms of beginnings and ends, an insoluble mystery.

With the development of modern physics, especially in the twentieth century, this mystery appears to have grown in complexity and scope. Relativistic physics no longer allows us to speak of time in a linear sense or of space in the three-dimensional way in which most people understand it. These new frontiers in science, particularly in cosmology, however, call into question the notion of infinite regression in time, which throws an even greater challenge to the basic idea of the cosmological argument.

If we turn in the other direction and introduce the reality of God to account for the existence of the universe, we are once more caught in perplexity. Creation *ex nihilo*, that is, creation out of nothing, is not an easy idea to handle, if nothing else because nothing in our experience can be used as a point of reference to make sense of it. Things come from things, ideas from ideas, conditions from conditions, animals from animals, people from people, but nothing comes from nothing. How, then, is it possible for the world to have emerged out of nothing? What rational sense can we make of such an origination, even if we presuppose a divine cause for it? Furthermore, if God existed before the world, there was really no nothing, and we might have to believe, as some philosophers and theologians do, that it is not that God created the world out of nothing but out of himself. From this point of view, the world is an emanation, a transformation, or rather a deformation of God. In these considerations, however, we have strayed far from the path of reason and have entered the domain of faith, which is not what we sought to do by an appeal to a rational argument such as the cosmological argument.

There is also another disturbing thought. If the first premise of this argument states that everything must have a necessary cause, must we not ask about God the same question that is relevant to the existence of the world? Why, after all, does God exist? Two alternatives lie in front of us: we either affirm that God is the uncaused cause of the world, or believe, as the ancient Greeks did with respect to their gods, that one god came from another god who came from another and so on for all eternity. The second alternative involves us again in an endless chain of regression that leads to a mysterious abyss about which reason has nothing to say. The first alternative does not fare much better. An uncaused first cause is as enigmatic a concept as can be imagined, which leads us to the last argument of theism that, as a conclusion, we will consider briefly.

Known as the ontological argument and made famous by a passage from the writings of Saint Anselm of Canterbury, this argument remains a classic in philosophy. Viewed by some as only a linguistic game and regarded by others as a compelling line of reasoning, the ontological argument deserves consideration. The word 'ontological' is derived from the Greek word *on* that conveys the sense of 'what exists' or 'what is'. The ontological argument has been expressed in various forms, in one of which we find it in the following formulation: (1) God is by definition a being anything greater than which cannot be conceived; (2) a being anything greater than which cannot be conceived is by definition a perfect being; (3) perfection is a notion that conveys the presence of all possible attributes; (4) existence is an attribute; (5) therefore existence must be attributed to God, which means, clearly, that God exists.

Let us note that unlike in the previous arguments, we do not proceed here from an examination of the world to the existence of God, but from an analysis of the definition of the concept of God to his existence. All that we need to know is this definition, and from this knowledge we can only conclude that God must exist. Hence, to deny his existence entails a misunderstanding of what 'God' means, for which reason Saint Anselm repeats the biblical line quoted earlier: only a fool —that is, someone who does not understand the meanings of words—can deny the existence of God, which would be equivalent to not understanding, for instance, that 'triangle' means 'a three-angle figure'. By definition, then, the word 'God' entails perfection, and perfection implies existence, which amounts to saying that the statement 'God exists' is a tautology, that is, a statement that merely clarifies the meaning of a term. We can put the matter differently. The essence of God, which is what the definition expresses, implies his existence. A nonexisting God would turn out to be a contradiction in terms, as would a four-angle triangle, and only fools speak in this way.

Several important components of the argument, however, present conceptual difficulties. The first premise calls for our accepting a definition of God as a being anything greater than which cannot be conceived. Nothing greater, nothing more sublime, nothing more perfect can even be imagined, for the idea of God surpasses by far anything that could enter our minds. In this sense, therefore, God is beyond every limit both in the world and in what we can think about the world. But, as noted earlier, a definition that excludes all limits is one that fails to fulfill its task of defining its subject, for to define means to impose a limit. Furthermore, the greater the limits imposed by a definition, the more clearly its subject is, and, on the reverse side, the fewer the limits, the more unclear the subject. If, however, we insist on removing all limits, as when we speak of a being anything greater than which cannot be conceived, then from a rational point of view the meaning of our definition dissipates into nothing. For can the mind truly grasp the essence of that beyond which nothing can be thought?

There is also the issue of the legitimacy of deriving the idea of existence from the notion of perfection. This notion, as understood by Saint Anselm, implies completeness or fullness, which is what the Latin word *perfectio* means. A perfect piano is one from which nothing that is supposed to belong to a piano is missing. The question is whether an existing piano is more perfect than an imaginary piano precisely because it exists. It has been repeatedly argued by the critics of the ontological argument that perfection is *not* a quality and is *not* something that we can add to the definition of anything. Things can be defined adequately even if they do not exist, as when we define a unicorn as a horse endowed with a horn. Moreover, there may be something related to the idea of perfection that can be even more damaging to the argument. A perfect piano does not exist anywhere except as an ideal construction among pianomakers, because as soon as this construction becomes embodied in matter, it is bound to be less than perfect, as defects and shortcomings do not fail to appear. Hence, perfection and existence, both in the physical world and in any other world, are mutually exclusive ideas for which reason certain Oriental religions see in nonexistence—*nirvana*—the ultimate state of perfection: to be absolutely nothing is preferable to any state of existence, for existence is always tainted with imperfection. But if this is so, the ontological argument can be turned around to demonstrate that God, because of his perfection, cannot exist: the essence of God entails his being absolutely nothing.

If, however, we are unwilling to go to this extreme, we may say that all that can be shown in this argument is that the world, understood in the sense of the totality of being, exists, because only the idea of the world can approximate the definition of God given in the first premise, that is, anything greater than which cannot be conceived. In this case, we would find ourselves supporting pantheism, a view which equates God with the world but which deprives the concept of God of some of the most important attributes that theism associates with it, such as omniscience and benevolence. If, as Spinoza contended, God and the world are the same, would it make sense to pray to God or to regard him as the provident protector of human beings?

The key that allows us to understand and appreciate the ontological argument, no less than other arguments for the existence of God, is the realization that in *all* of them what we find is a philosophical exercise in which an already accepted faith is engaged in making sense of itself—faith seeking understanding. If that faith is absent, the demonstrative knowledge of God is only an illusion, and nothing, absolutely nothing, can possibly convince us of God's existence. This is perhaps the reason why fideism insists that faith, and faith alone, is the only avenue that supports the human belief in God. Something similar can be said concerning arguments against the existence of God. In them, as in the argument from evil, we begin from the assumption that God does not exist and then proceed to identify facts and circumstances that support that assumption. Faith and reason may turn out to be two disparate ways of looking at the world that cannot enter into a meaningful dialogue. From the perspective of reason, faith is a mystery that defies a final solution, but from the point of view of faith, reason may not be more than a distraction, sometimes useful, sometimes detrimental, that reduces reality to a rational dimension and may not be more than a simplification of what is real.

As one considers all that has been said and written about God in religion, in philosophy, and in ordinary human discourse, it is difficult to avoid the temptation of concluding that it all may amount to a series of efforts to confront a reality that could have little in common with what human beings have thought and believed about the matter. What lies beneath the controversies that the concept of God has given rise to among philosophers and among ordinary people is the most difficult, yet perhaps the most critical, aspect of the philosophical adventure, namely, one's conception of reality. We will now explore this aspect in the concluding chapter, and we will see how this conception has been interpreted and defended by various philosophers.

# Chapter 6

# The Quest for Reality

There is a story in Plato's *Republic* with which we can begin these concluding reflections on the adventure of philosophy, where we will explore the most difficult yet the most exciting part of our journey—the quest for reality. As in most of his other dialogues, Plato speaks to us in the *Republic* through Socrates, and often does so in myths and allegories that serve the purpose of illustrating and rendering accessible to us his deepest philosophical convictions. As if to open for us a window into his understanding of reality and knowledge, that is, his metaphysics and epistemology, he entertains us with a tale about certain people who live in an underground cave where they have been since birth and which they call their world, because they have never been anywhere else. In this dark cave, they lie chained to its bottom by heavy fetters, which, however, they do not recognize as chains because they have always been constrained by them. To appreciate freedom it is necessary to have been enslaved at least once, and to understand slavery it is essential to have been free. We grasp the significance of concepts only by contrasts, and for this reason the inhabitants of the cave are not even aware of being in a cave, for they know nothing else. Their chains are for them only natural conditions. They are prisoners in a cave, yet they are not aware that they are. Behind them, and unknown to them, there is a fire on a platform casting a dim light. In front of the fire, there are strange people who, again unnoticed by the prisoners, move from one side to the other, carrying objects in their hands and emitting sounds of all kinds. Against the light of the fire, the objects cast huge and blurry shadows on the wall that lies in front of the prisoners, and the echo of the cave projects the sounds onto the wall creating the impression that it is the shadows that emit them.

There, in the cave, the prisoners live and die, unaware of their chains, of the fire and the moving objects, and, above all, of the cave in which they are imprisoned. The cave, they think, is the world, and the blurry and talking shadows are reality. What else could we expect of people who have lived in chains and have known and experienced nothing else? Never having been outside of the cave or having even heard about a world beyond the cave, how could they not equate their experiences with reality and their unfortunate fate with what is and should be normal? To pass the time and make sense of what they see and hear, the prisoners invent games and diversions among themselves, assign names to the shadows that move in front of them, and even develop theories about them, arranging them in sequences and awarding prizes and rewards to those who remember the greatest number of shadows and identify them by their right names. 'Name that shadow', 'Explain that shadow', and 'Predict the next shadow' are their favorite games, except, of course, that they do not speak of shadows but of things, because the idea of a shadow does not exist for someone who has only seen shadows. Those who excel in these games are called sophists and scientists and people of great knowledge, and those who either do poorly in the games or pay no attention to the shadows they call ignorant and mindless.

At some point and for unknown reasons, one of the prisoners breaks his chains and begins to walk about the cave, clumsily and painfully at first because his limbs are not used to movement. Untouched by the jeers and sneers of his fellow prisoners who look upon him as a demented man, he walks toward the back of the cave and climbs onto the platform where he sees the fire and the people who carry the objects and make the noises that create the talking shadows. It takes him some time to get accustomed to the light of the fire, for he has never seen light before, but at last he inspects the scene and understands what the shadows are and how unfortunate he has been to mistake them for reality. Not the shadows, he says, but these moving objects constitute the real world. Somehow, however, he sees yet another fire, a light that dimly illuminates the mouth of the cave, and, impelled by a mysterious impulse, he begins his ascent out of the cave. This ascent, Plato tells us, is rugged and steep and fraught with dangers and aggravations, but this does not dissuade the liberated prisoner. He climbs and falls, and climbs and falls again, until at last he finds himself in the world outside. What a wonderful sight, he thinks, and yet how painful! His eyes, accustomed to the darkness of the cave, can hardly see anything at first, and all in him is confusion and anguish, for he has never experienced such things. He struggles against the temptation to crawl back into his underground abode but chooses to stay in his newly discovered world. In time, his sight grows accustomed to the light and he begins to identify the objects that surround him: a tree here, a hill in the distance, a lake in the vicinity. He notices that he can see more clearly the reflections of objects on water than the objects themselves, but in time he has the courage to fix his eyes on the objects themselves. If the fire in the cave, he asks himself, made the objects carried by the people on the platform visible and the shadows of those objects possible, what could make the objects in the outside world possible and visible? Hence, his eyes look for the great fire outside the cave, until he discovers the sun, which, however, cannot be seen directly, for its light is too intense, but which, he concludes, must be taken for granted as the source of light and as the supporter of all that world.

At that moment, he remembers his old habitation and his fellow prisoners. Could it be, he wonders, that they have never heard of an outside world? Could they imagine that the dancing shadows that flicker on the wall of the cave are real? Moved by compassion and by a desire to spread the news to those who live in darkness, the liberated prisoner begins his descent into the cave. He finds himself once more facing the shadows that he now knows are only illusions and tells his neighbors what he has seen outside. But 'outside' is an unknown word among them, and so are 'fire', 'reflections on water', and other similar terms. His speech is incomprehensible. His tale makes no sense. His joy is unexplainable. "Up you went and down you came without your brain," they shout to him. Eventually, they manage to silence him by death, because his presence is an intolerable annoyance that would not allow them to observe in peace the moving shadows.

The meaning of Plato's allegory of the cave, as this story is known, has been interpreted in various ways, although its extraordinary significance has been generally recognized. Schopenhauer, for instance, spoke of it as the most important passage in the history of philosophy, and few are those who have not seen in it a compelling statement, not only of Plato's metaphysics but also of the meaning of the philosophical adventure. It contains many symbols, which, like arrows, point in visual ways to the concepts and principles that are at the heart of the human quest for reality. The cave obviously symbolizes the physical world, which sense experience reveals. The shadows represent the impressions that we receive through the senses, and the fire is a symbol for the sun, through the power and light of which the physical world sustains itself and is visible. The chains that bind the prisoners stand for the physical and social limitations within which human beings live, and the passage that leads out of the cave is an image for philosophy, understood as a process in which we grow in understanding and clarity of mind. The world outside the cave represents what Plato believed to be true reality, and the sun is a symbol for what he called the Idea of the Good, the highest reality, and what renders it intelligible and rational. The prisoner who escapes from the cave and who returns to it to spread the good news to his fellow prisoners is a metaphor for the philosopher—perhaps Socrates, who, like the prisoner, paid with his life for his own liberation. There are still other symbols and images, such as the reflections of objects on water, all of which together form one of the most powerful allegories in philosophy. From Plato himself we learn the meanings of some of the symbols and, above all, the overall significance of the allegory of the cave. He tells us that it is a representation of the human condition and that it is we who are the prisoners.

Elsewhere in the *Republic*, Plato furnishes us, again from Socrates' mouth, with a complementary image, the line of knowledge in which we learn that knowledge is comparable to an unequally divided and ascending line. Its lower part, also divided into two unequal sections, represents dreams and illusions at the bottom and sense perceptions at the top. Both sections symbolize the domain of opinion where neither truth nor certainty can be found. In the higher part of the line, we come upon divisions, which, in ascending order, stand for the objects of mathematics, the Ideal Forms, and the Idea of the Good. It is here, and only here, that true knowledge is found. This image of the line of knowledge is a metaphor that sheds light on Plato's epistemology, just as the story of the cave is an allegory that explains in visual language his metaphysics. The allegory of the cave and the image of the line of knowledge go together because they address areas of philosophical concern that are inseparable, namely, how we understand the idea of reality and how we explain the process of knowledge. Our understanding of what is real is conditioned by the way in which we conceive of knowledge, and our explanation of knowledge depends on our conception of reality.

The word 'metaphysics' has a curious origin. Among the surviving works of Aristotle, there is one entitled the *Physics* in which he gives an account of the processes of nature that the Greeks called *physis*, that is, the changes and regularities of the physical world. Another work, possibly written after the *Physics*, was apparently left untitled or was found by a late editor of Aristotle's books without a title. The editor, a scholar named Andronicus of Rhodes (first century B.C.) called it the *After-or-beyond-the-Physics*, a title expressed in Greek by the phrase *meta ta physica*, from which the word 'metaphysics' is derived. The word *meta* is a Greek preposition that means 'after', as when something is said to have happened *after* something else, or 'about', as when we talk *about* a subject. It also conveys the sense of 'beyond', as when we speak of God as being *beyond* the world. Possibly, the editor of Aristotle's books used the word *meta* to express these meanings: written *after* the *Physics*, the untitled book became the *After-the-Physics*, and dealing with a subject that is in some sense *beyond* the physical world, there was justification in calling it the *Beyond-or-about-the-Physical-World*.

What is important for us, however, is to have some idea about the subjects with which Aristotle deals in his *Metaphysics*. This work, one of the most complex in the history of writing, deals with many issues including cosmological and astronomical matters (the oldest estimate of the circumference of the earth is found in it), but there are two issues that are recurrent: (1) the nature and sources of knowledge and (2) the meanings of certain universal concepts by reference to which the world can be explained. Among these, for instance, we find matter, form, time, space, cause, purpose, relationship, quality, quantity, and others. These concepts are the foundation of the sciences (which Aristotle sought to classify), as well as of the structure of language and thought. But possibly of greater significance is another issue discussed in the *Metaphysics* that takes us to the core of metaphysics understood in a philosophical sense,[1] namely, the meaning of reality.

Through the senses, we become initially aware of the existence of things and of ourselves as physical objects. Eventually, through the use of the mind and with the aid of imagination, other things make themselves present in our consciousness in the form of ideas, fictions, possibilities, expectations, and countless other things, all of which, we conclude, also exist alongside physical things, but, we suspect, in different ways. The world, too, exists as a totality of all these things, whether physical or otherwise, and we are part of this collection of existing things. Vaguely, we are aware that there are different kinds or levels of existence. There are, of course, things that we can see and touch, and these undoubtedly exist and are real, and if there are doubts about their existence, all we have to do is to appeal to our senses to confirm their reality. They all, however, exist only for some time and are always undergoing changes so that what they are today is not what they were yesterday or what they will be tomorrow. Eventually, they will disappear from our immediate awareness and will be replaced by other things, leaving behind only memories. Their temporary reality is made possible by their relative permanence and is somehow a function of how seemingly stable or durable they are.

Nevertheless, memories also exist as long as they are present in the mind, and so do thoughts, images, dreams, hallucinations, fears, aspirations, and all sorts of others things, the reality of which cannot be denied. And aside from these, still other kinds of things also exist on other levels. There are numbers and formulas, laws of nature, logical principles, and an infinity of other objects, most of which are neither immediately accessible to the senses nor are caught in the wheel of time like those that belong to the physical world. Moreover, if we take into account the objects of faith, beginning with God and the human soul, then the inventory of existing things reveals itself as truly extraordinary both in extent and in complexity. God and the soul exist, says the believer, and so do other invisible and immaterial things, all of which share existence and reality with galaxies, stars, atoms, trees, people, dreams, irrational numbers, geometrical theorems, and multitudes of other things. If we are justified in affirming that they exist on some level and in some fashion and that they are real in one way or another, we must be able to raise two

---

1. Metaphysics is sometimes understood in other ways. There is, for instance, the sense in which it stands for the study of or the preoccupation with dimensions of reality that are only marginally related to the physical world. Spiritualism, ghost-seeing, reincarnation, out-of-body experiences, the occult, and other similar things are often said to be 'metaphysical' matters. This, however, is *not* the sense in which, from a philosophical point of view, metaphysics should be understood.

questions: (1) How do we know that anything is real? and (2) What do we mean when we say that something exists? The first of these questions is basic in epistemology, while the second is the subject-matter of metaphysics. They are inseparable, because in answering either one of them we address the other. How we interpret the process of knowledge determines how we understand the meaning of reality, and what reality means for us conditions our view of knowledge.

As with questions about moral values and the existence of God, we soon find that regarding questions about knowledge and reality, philosophers have proposed many answers that range from complex systems of ideas, as we encounter in Plato and Aristotle, to a turning away from such questions as if they were not only unanswerable but meaningless and useless. They say that whenever philosophers began to raise metaphysical questions, Diogenes would invariably walk away, which was his way of answering those questions. We can sympathize with his impatience with philosophical discussions that take us away from the world of physical things and from sense experience, because that world and that experience are for most of us what we mean by reality. Is not a bad toothache more real than all the speculations and theories of those philosophers who allege to have discovered true reality in some immaterial and transcendent world? The way in which some religious people conduct themselves and live their lives reveals with clarity the fact that, despite their faith in God and in the immortality of the soul, it is their bodies and the physical world that command their allegiance, because for them, as for most people, things ready-at-hand are more real than anything else. Still, regardless of how entrenched we may be in the physical world and how attached we may be to practical concerns, it is unavoidable that at least occasionally questions about reality are bound to emerge. The natural need to make sense of things compels some people to come to grips with such questions, and it is then that the problem of reality presents itself as a problem that demands a solution.

To the question "What is reality?" many answers are possible. We can say, for instance, that reality is precisely what sense experience reveals and that what exists is independent of the mind. If there were no consciousness to perceive and know the world, the world would remain exactly as it is and always has been, for its existence does not depend on and is not affected by the knower, that is, by the mind. Time and space, colors and smells, sounds and textures would all remain the same if there were no one to observe or measure them. The example of a tree that falls in a forest illustrates this point. If a tree falls in a remote forest where there is nobody to witness the event, would the tree make a noise as it hits the ground? Metaphysical objectivism replies that whether or not there is a sensing ear to hear the noise, there is a noise just the same, only that it is not *heard*. Thus, noise, tree, forest, and every physical thing in the world would be unaffected by the absence of an observer, just as before sensing organisms came into existence and after they will become extinct, things were and will remain as they are. Time goes on passing and space is the same, whether or not a conscious being is present. Stated differently, we could say that we, as conscious beings endowed with the capacity to perceive and think, exist in the world and are part of a cosmic reality just as any other physical thing. Through the senses, the world reflects itself on the mind, which is like a mirror on which an object is reflected. If the mirror breaks, the image disappears, but the object remains intact. After my death, when my consciousness will cease experiencing the world, things will continue to exist. Other people will inhabit my house and make use of my things, winter will arrive as it always does in December, flowers will bloom in the spring, the leaves will fall in autumn, celebrations and games will take place, the earth will go on orbiting the sun. In sum, nothing will really change, because the world is not affected by my awareness of it. More precisely, the *object of knowledge*—the world—is not contingent on the *subject of knowledge*—the mind. On the contrary, the mind depends on the world, for if the world did not exist, or if it had evolved differently, there would be no mind or, at least, it would be different from what it is.

Metaphysical objectivism has had powerful supporters. There is, on the one hand, the support that comes from common sense and from what we might call animal faith, that is, the instinctual and natural way in which the ordinary consciousness interprets reality. Physical objects stand before us as we perceive them but are unaffected when we move away. Could I imagine that my room ceases to exist when I walk out or that things disappear when I forget about them? Who would think that time does not pass if we fail to keep track of its passing or that space does not exist unless it is measured or that the days of the week would not follow one another if nobody were aware of them? The year when I was born is precisely that year, irrespective of my birth, and stars and galaxies exist in space even if no eyes, human or otherwise, were there to see them. Common sense, then, recognizes the permanence of things, the reality of matter, and the structure of the world and concludes that the presence of a mind is *not* an essential component in the equation of reality. What is, is, because it is, not because it is perceived or conceived by the mind.

There is, on the other hand, support from philosophers such as Aristotle, for whom existence belongs to physical things, which he conceived of in terms of the union of a certain amount of matter and a specific form. Unformed matter, that is, matter without shape or form, is only an idea, a concept in the mind, and so is immaterial form, that is, form that is devoid of material content. A living cat exists and is a living cat because of the union of a certain matter and a certain form. A different matter would result in a plastic cat, a painted cat, or some other type of cat, and a different form would produce something other than a cat, for instance, a dog. This view of things is called hylomorphism, a term derived from the Greek words for 'matter' (*hyle*) and 'form' (*morphe*). It insists that reality must be primarily understood in terms of things (matter *and* form) and that anything else must be seen as functions of things. For example, dreams, imaginations, emotions, relations, ideas, and thoughts exist but only because they are either 'accidents' that happen to things or products of a consciousness that creates them. This consciousness, however, exists *in* a physical body, not as a ghost inside a machine but as a function of that body. No body equals no consciousness.[2] From this point of view, then, the question concerning the nature of existence is answered by affirming the reality of the world of concrete things revealed through sense perception, which is itself also a physical process. Things exist because they are transformations of the matter that constitutes the world, more precisely the *arche* that the Presocratics postulated as the basis of reality.

Other manifestations of metaphysical objectivism can be adduced. In all of them, we come upon the conviction that reality is independent of consciousness and that what the senses perceive is, in principle, real. We say in principle, because unrefined and uncritical sense perception cannot give us a faithful representation of the way things really are. In chapter 2, we quoted a line from the fragments of Heraclitus that tells us that the senses are bad witnesses, and they certainly are. How many times, indeed, they can mislead us! What we see and hear often turns out to be different from what, after further inspection, we recognize as real, and we know that what exists is more complex than what we perceive. Intellectual growth consists in the capacity to take into account what is known through sense experience and to subject it to examination in order to avoid confusing what appears with what is and in order to arrive at a more truthful idea of the world. Still, if we are convinced that reality is objective in the sense of not being dependent on the mind, we must accept sense experience as the first door through which we must pass to gain entrance into reality. Without sense experience, no knowledge is possible and no understanding of reality is conceivable. For this reason, empiricism is a view that is generally found among the advocates of metaphysical objectivism.

The word 'empiricism' is derived from the Greek word for 'experience' (*empeiria*). Empirical knowledge, accordingly, is the knowledge that comes to us directly through sense experience. The colors we see, the textures we touch, the sounds we hear, the shapes we recognize, the flavors we taste—all this is empirical

---

2. Great efforts have been made by commentators of Aristotle, such as Saint Thomas Aquinas, to interpret his hylomorphism in a way that allows for the existence of immaterial reality (e.g., God and the soul). The issue is, of course, not closed, and it remains true that different interpretations of Aristotle's metaphysics are possible. Still, I am inclined to agree with those who fail to detect in him any trace of a belief that immaterial things can truly exist.

knowledge and is something we share with animals, for they, too, sense things around them. As we grow up, we construct our idea of the world out of our sensations, and through memory and imagination we extend and refine this construction. Eventually, with the aid of language and further mental development, we form ideas and invent concepts, some of them far removed from what the senses originally supply to us but all of them rooted in experience. The capacity to think is not something that we share with animals, for it appears to be a unique human endowment. Animals can neither talk nor think and are, as far as we can tell, mostly confined to their immediate experiences. Still, regardless of how advanced we may be in our capacity to think, empiricism insists that it is with sense experience that all knowledge begins and that sense experience is the final test to which all knowledge must be subjected. Locke, for instance, argued that the human mind is originally a blank slate, a *tabula rasa*, on which nothing is found until sense experience 'writes' on it and forms in it impressions that are the building blocks of all subsequent knowledge. Imagine a child who is born without the ability to see, hear, taste, or touch anything. What would that child know about himself or about the world? Would not his mind be empty of all knowledge? In the absence of innate or inborn ideas, which empiricism regards as fictions, he would have no knowledge at all and no language, which is also learned in experience.

In Aristotle's *Metaphysics*, this explanation of the origin of human knowledge is outlined. For him, we begin with simple sensations and we move from these to memories and anticipations, and from them, with the aid of language, to concepts and theories. A concept is a word under which we group a collection of experiences. Take, for instance, the word 'school'. It allows us to identify a vast number of experiences and derivations from experiences such as memories and imaginations. It includes my elementary school with its building, furniture, teachers, children, books, games, good and bad recollections, and other similar things. It also includes other schools, not only mine, and Plato's Academy and various schools of philosophy about which I may have learned from books, and schools of fish, and countless other instances identified by this simple word. A word, accordingly, is worth a thousand images, not the reverse, as is often maintained, for which reason language is essential in the process of thinking and is an indication of a person's intelligence. We think in terms of concepts and systems of concepts, which we call theories. Concepts are, then, words that permit us to gather experiences for the purpose of retaining them in memory and communicating them to others. This explains why only after language is available to a child, is he able to remember. Thought and language are, therefore, coextensive and coexisting.

After Aristotle and in part because of him, the empirical tradition has remained important in the development of philosophy and fundamental in the growth of the sciences, all of which insist in one way or another that knowledge begins with experience, and that truth can only be found by testing theories and hypotheses in the light of observation. After Francis Bacon in the sixteenth century, the idea that knowledge can be obtained independently of sense experience has been progressively abandoned in the sciences. In his view, the theories of his predecessors did not amount to much, precisely because of their belief, especially among medieval philosophers, that reality can be known by merely thinking about reality or by creating ideas that are unrelated to the world unveiled by the senses. With Bacon, the path followed by the sciences, initially the physical sciences and later on the social sciences, was clearly outlined. First we must *see* the world and then form hypotheses and theories that must be tested and retested through further observations. Whatever transcends the realm of what is observable, whatever contradicts experience, whatever defies verification through observation is only a collection of intellectual cobwebs that philosophers spin out of their imagination. What would astronomy be if human beings were not endowed with eyesight? What knowledge of the planets and the stars and of the universe at large could have been possible? When in 1610 Galileo turned the first telescope toward the sky, all he did was to extend his eyesight by means of technology, and the knowledge that he acquired in the process was nothing but extended sense perception. This allowed him to impel astronomy toward a more comprehensive understanding of the physical world and, thereby, of reality itself.

Many philosophers have chosen the path outlined by Bacon. Locke, as we have seen, dismissed innate or inborn ideas and limited knowledge to what sense experience discloses. This empirical tradition gained further support from philosophers such as Hume, who, again, brushed aside the claim that sense experience is only a source of illusion. The shadows that the prisoners of Plato's cave contemplate, he would have said, *are* what is real, because it is what the senses reveal. This marriage between knowledge and sense experience, generally accepted in the name of common sense, has been enthroned by modern science as an indisputable fact, and what is regarded as the triumph of science over nature, that is, its ability to control the world, is adduced as proof that reality is what the senses disclose.

In recent times, a further development in this direction has taken place. The metaphysical concerns of ancient and medieval philosophers, and of their descendants in early modern times, which dealt with questions about the meaning of reality and about the nature of the human soul, have been bracketed away not only by the empirically driven sciences but even by philosophy itself. From this point of view, everything must be reduced to what is knowable and verifiable in and through sense experience. If no empirical verification is possible concerning an issue, it must be meaningless and must be treated as fiction and myth. This point has been made by logical positivism (also known as scientific empiricism), a twentieth-century movement in philosophy that maintains that factual statements that are not verifiable through observation are not only neither true nor false but meaningless. Thus, for instance, statements such as 'God exists', 'a spiritual self lies at the basis of experience', 'time is an illusion', and other similar 'metaphysical' statements, are as meaningless as the statement 'number twenty will marry an orange yesterday'. In this bizarre statement, language is used without conveying any sense, because nothing can possibly be constructed as the basis for verifying or falsifying what it purports to say.

In empiricism, then, sense experience not only sets the parameters of reality but draws the boundaries of the meaningfulness of language, which, translated into ordinary speech, means that we can only talk about what can be perceived, because there is nothing aside from what the senses disclose. Even consciousness itself—the soul, which Socrates identified with genuine reality—is eliminated from the vocabulary of science and of much contemporary philosophy as if it were an embarrassing fiction. The self, for instance in behaviorism, can only be understood in terms of observable behavioral responses and actions. In the statement 'I love you', there is neither an 'I' who loves nor a 'you' who is loved but only a series of situations and acts that are what the statement means. If these cannot be described in perceptible terms, the statement lacks meaning and is only a series of sounds. The same can be said with respect to statements that claim to say something about God, the soul, the freedom of the will, moral values, and all similar things through which we *appear* to be saying something but in which we are not saying anything at all.

This attitude that reduces reality to the realm of what is observable and that proclaims science, which invariably follows an empirical track, as the key to reality, is sometimes referred to as scientism, a term used sometimes in a negative sense by those who have misgivings about the claim that science alone can disclose reality. It is also used by those who discern in empiricism a commitment to metaphysical materialism, a view that presents to us a picture of reality in which existence is limited to the physical or material world. Only material things exist, and anything that supposedly transcends the material world is either a fiction or a second-class reality explainable in terms of a physical object. In materialism, reality and the material world are one. Neither a transcendent God nor an immortal soul nor anything of the sort can be conceived of as existing except as ideas in the mind, which is itself a physiological product of a material object—the human brain.

The connection between empiricism and materialism is not difficult to understand. The former is an epistemological view that limits knowledge to what is observable, and the latter is a metaphysical idea that affirms the exclusive existence of matter, which is what sense perception reveals. It is the matter of which a table is made that lets me see and touch it, because my senses are the physiological antennae with which my body—a material object—perceives the world. An immaterial table is an intangible object that I cannot know, because it has no matter. Furthermore, a material table exists independently of my awareness of it. Whether I sense it or not, it remains in existence, because reality does not depend on consciousness. Hence, metaphysical objectivism stands related to empiricism and materialism and forms with them a basic approach to the question of the nature of reality. As we have noted, common sense supports it and the progress of modern science gives ample testimony of the success with which it serves as the most sensible explanation of the world. In its presence, Plato's allegory of the cave turns out to be a fiction that misunderstands the meaning of reality. There is no cave, nor are there prisoners nor shadows nor a need to escape to a world above nor anything of the sort. What the so-called prisoners see in front of them are not shadows but the real objects of sense experience, and their talk about them, which Plato regards as language games about shadows, is, at least at times, genuine discourse about what is real. Those who, like Plato, speak of other dimensions beyond the physical world—a world outside the cave—are dreamers who have let their imagination fly away on the wings of illusions of no substance. The quest of reality, the goal of metaphysics, should be directed at the world disclosed by sense experience, as Aristotle insisted. If the 'shadows' are blurry and unstable, it is only because the material world is always changing and because the senses are imperfect and often unreliable.

This last statement gives us a hint concerning the problem inherent in metaphysical objectivism and concerning the reasons why some philosophers have chosen other paths. If the material world is always in a state of flux, as Heraclitus noted, is it at all possible that when we see an object we only perceive an illusory state of permanence? Guided by what the senses disclose, we could not say that anything is anything, because Being—what truly is—requires permanence and stability, but these are conditions not found in the material world. All material things, including our bodies, are caught in the maddening wheel of time, which constantly turns them from what they were into what they are and from what they are into what they will be, like the changing waters of a river, which are never the same. Can we, then, insist on attributing reality to *this* world and reliability to our physical senses? Should we not, on the contrary, close our eyes to this world of change and uncertainty and search for reality in an altogether different direction? But what other direction could there be? Is it not possible to conclude that since permanence cannot be found in the material world, and neither can certainty be expected from sense experience, we should assume a stance of skepticism, like that of Pyrrho and the Sophists, and say that there is nothing at all to be known, really known, about anything? Possibly, we live in a cave in which we are condemned to look at shadows and phantoms, but this cave has no exit, and even if it did, what guarantee would there be that it may not lead to yet another cave? Escaping from this cave, then, would merely entail falling into another set of shadows and illusions. This is a distressing prospect but a real one. It would mean that the quest for reality is bound to be futile, and neither about the material world nor about any other world, is any knowledge possible. Somehow, we have come into existence as conscious beings out of an eternity of unconsciousness, and in no time we will return to that eternity without the slightest clue about who or what we are or why or for what purpose we have emerged from nothing into something, only to return to nothing.

The distrust toward the claims of metaphysical objectivism and its corollaries (empiricism and materialism) has a double source. There is, on the one hand, the realization that sense experience is often unreliable and always subjective, and, on the other, there is the difficulty of defining the concept of matter independently of perception. It is easy to show that our senses frequently deceive us. What we see is at times different from what proves to be real, and there are experiences that, while similar to perceptions, come from within the mind and are only mental phenomena. Dreams and imaginations, for instance, resemble perceptions and yet do not disclose actual things, a circumstance that led Descartes to entertain the *possibility* that what we normally call reality and the world of dreams are one and the same thing. Reality, then, turns out to be a mental construction and the external or objective world a product of the mind. As Schopenhauer expressed it, the world is ultimately only *my* representation, a series of mental images that are a function of *my* consciousness. It first came into existence when I became aware of it, remains in existence so long as my awareness of it remains, and becomes nothing as soon as I cease to exist. Not only will I not be able to attend my own funeral, my funeral will simply not exist at all. As a series of experiences, the world will prove to be a brief dream, unless I manage to survive my death as a disembodied spirit.

Besides the lack of reliability of sense experience, there is the difficulty of defining matter independently of perception. A table is a physical object. But what does this mean? It means that it has a color, a shape, and a structure and is made of some material like wood. Still, what are these qualities except perceptions in my mind? Is not color the sensation of color or shape the awareness of shape? And as for a material substance that underlies these qualities—what in the context of the Presocratics is called *arche*—what else could it be but a conceptual fiction created by the mind to find something on which to attach qualities? Ultimately, then, matter, which from the perspective of metaphysical objectivism is the basis of reality, may be nothing more than a complex of experienced qualities with no reality of its own except that which stems from a consciousness that is aware of it. But if this is so, must we not conclude that instead of saying that the mind exists in the world, it is the world that exists in the mind and only in the mind? Things do not exist in time and space, as common sense contends, and neither do time and space exist in things, as Aristotle maintained. The fact is that both time and space, and things and the world at large, are only mental occurrences, not substantially different from dreams and thoughts. To return to the allegory of the cave: subjective idealism (or metaphysical subjectivism), as this view is known, would say that the cave with its shadows, fire, and moving objects exists only in the consciousness of the prisoners. This includes the outside world. Everything is a grand and mysterious mental reality with no basis outside the mind. Literally, as we move away from metaphysical objectivism toward subjective idealism, we witness a process whereby the mind swallows the entire world until it is reduced to a mental image.

There have been many advocates of subjective idealism throughout the history of philosophy, and as a disturbing possibility, it has been entertained by practically every person at one time or another. Occasionally, we all suspect that time is not as real as is normally believed, that things change as our awareness of them changes, that reality is not quite like a solid brick that lies in front of us but is rather an elastic presence that molds itself in accordance with our moods and states of mind, and that, in sum, the world exists in us, not we in the world. Taken to an extreme, this suspicion leads to solipsism (from the Latin words *solus* and *ipsus*, 'alone' and 'by itself'). The solipsist believes that only his consciousness exists, and that, therefore, the world (including other people) is only an occurrence in his mind, once more not unlike a dream. Would a personal tragedy, an accident, a terrible disease, or any other similar situation convince the solipsist that his mind is *not* the only real thing? Would an angry dog running after the solipsist prove to him that besides him there is at least something else, namely, the angry dog? Probably not, because he may retort that such occurrences are segments of the dream or, rather, of the nightmare that exists only in his mind. Solipsism, as a philosophical position, is rare. Schopenhauer once said that confirmed cases of solipsism are found only in madhouses, where the concept of reality is as changeable and varied as the clouds in the sky. He adds, however, that, as a metaphysical view, solipsism is irrefutable, because no convincing arguments can be adduced to invalidate it. For the solipsist, neither the external world nor minds other than his own exist. For him, then, the entire cave and all other possible worlds are real only within himself and exist only as long as they are present in his consciousness.

Less extreme and more complex types of subjective idealism are often found among those philosophers who have challenged the claim that assigns an objective reality to the material world. Among the Presocratics, there is the case of Parmenides, who stands in the history of ideas as the archenemy of empiricism. Sense perception, according to him, creates in the mind only an indistinct world of illusion and deception to which no truth can be attached. What we gather from the senses allows us to form only opinions of no value. Through sense experience, we mistakenly conclude that time and space are real, that material objects exist, and that movement and change actually occur. The truth is, however, quite different. The *real* world is one in which neither time nor space is real, in which matter does not exist, and in which neither change nor movement takes place. The way of truth, to use Parmenides' language, is vastly different from the way of opinion, which is what most people, including some philosophers, assume to be true understanding. What, then, is the way of truth?

From what we learn from Parmenides' poetical statement about it, it is a path that leads us to the realization that reality is one absolute unity that undergoes no changes or mutations, admits of no differentiations, is timeless, and cannot be known through the senses but is recognized only by pure thought. The only thing that we can say about it is that *it is* and *cannot not be*. Its real name is, therefore, 'It is'.[3] It cannot change, because change entails becoming something that it is not and ceasing to be what it was. Being, therefore, precludes the existence of nothing, for nothing cannot be. It cannot move either, because movement presupposes empty space, which is nothing, too, and which cannot be. Motionless and immutable, it simply *is*. By contrast, however, what we normally identify as reality is always in a state of flux, changing and moving from what is to what is not and from what is not to what is, which is plainly impossible. For this reason, what we call reality as we walk along the way of opinion cannot be reality but only a fantasy of colors, smells, textures, sounds, and shapes. The 'reality' in which most people live, Parmenides would have said, has no more substance than the shadows that Plato describes in the allegory of the cave.

This language is dense and perplexing, and we should not be blamed if we walked away from it, just as Diogenes did whenever philosophers spoke in that fashion. Still, if we did, we would be missing an opportunity to witness metaphysical speculation at its highest point and human thought struggling to make sense of experience. Whatever the meaning of Parmenides' conception of reality may be —and there is little agreement in this respect among scholars—one thing stands out with clarity: it is possible to raise fundamental questions about the accuracy of what in ordinary language goes by the name of reality, about the reliability of sense perception as the instrument of knowledge, about the relationship between truth and opinion, and about the role played by the mind in the structuring of reality. Concerning this last point, a statement of Parmenides ought to be borne in mind. According to him, Being—that is, reality—and thought are one. To be and to think

---

3. There is a parallelism between Parmenides' characterization of Being or reality and the biblical passage (Exodus 3:14) where God (Yahweh) presents himself to Moses as 'I am who am'.

are one and the same thing, and what is and what is thought form an absolute unity. What is not cannot be thought, and what cannot be thought cannot be.

Here, then, we find a bridge between our earlier discussion of the relationship between consciousness and the world on the one hand, and, on the other, the metaphysics of Parmenides. In metaphysical objectivism, as we have seen, the world exists independently of consciousness. Whether known or not, perceived or not, the world remains the same. Sense experience and thought merely allow the mind to perceive and know the world but have no role in structuring its reality. In metaphysical subjectivism, however, the mind assumes an active role in the process, and the world becomes what it is because the mind invests it with its reality. Nothing exists, therefore, apart from what is known, for which reason Parmenides insists that Being and thought are inseparable. Reality (the objective world) and consciousness (the subject that knows) are one and the same thing. This idea could lead to solipsism, a view in which reality becomes one with *my* awareness of it. *This*, however, is *not* the direction in which Parmenides intends to take us or the sense of Plato's metaphysical orientation. In Plato's allegory of the cave, there is an exit that leads from the cave to a world outside, from the world of illusion and opinion to the world of reality and truth, and this exit is accessible to my mind and to other minds. Otherwise, why would have the liberated prisoner returned to the cave to spread the good news about his discovery?

This discovery is made possible by the use of reason and by a critical examination of the information accessible through sense perception. Such information is unreliable and unstable, and the 'reality' that it discloses is only a collection of subjective perceptions that may or may not reflect something outside the mind. It is, then, literally, a fantasy, an illusion, that exists only as long as it is perceived. George Berkeley, a remarkable philosopher of the eighteenth century, expressed it clearly in the phrase *esse est percipi*, which means 'to be (or to exist) is to be perceived'. Things come into being only when they are perceived or sensed, and outside a consciousness that is aware of them, they are nothing. Thus, to return to our previous example, if a tree falls in a forest and there is no one to observe its fall, is there a noise? In opposition to metaphysical objectivism and to common sense, Berkeley's answer is that there is neither a noise, nor a tree, nor a forest, nor anything else, because there is no one in whose consciousness anything could emerge as reality. What we call things are only aggregates of *perceived* qualities such as color, sound, texture, and solidity. Matter itself, which in materialism is accepted as reality, is a mental construct that allows us to structure our perceptions. The relationships in which things *appear* to be connected with one another, such as time, space, causality, and arrangement, are products of the consciousness that perceives the world and injects order into it. Time does not pass if there is no mind to notice its passing. Would today be Monday, would this year be 1999, would the earth turn on its axis and move around the sun if there were no minds to keep track of time? Would people stand related to one another in terms of 'realities', such as families, nations, political parties, systems of law, moral values, and the other relationships of social life, if there were no conscious human beings? What, then, would the world of ordinary experience be in a mindless world? Berkeley's answer would be the same—nothing at all, because all such things are only the creations of consciousness. If all human consciousness were to disappear and human beings were converted into robots, the world would cease to exist—the human world. But do we exist in any other world, or are we aware of any reality other than that which *we* have constructed?

There is, however, an element in Berkeley's metaphysics that must be emphasized, lest we conclude that he fell into the temptation of solipsism. The statement *esse est percipi* reduces the external world to a series of mental images and constructs, and a consciousness is required for the world to exist. Yet, we must ask, what consciousness and whose consciousness? If the answer is *my* consciousness alone, we are back in solipsism and the world exists only for me, a rare view that, on reflection, makes little sense. It is true that I am only directly aware of my awareness. I cannot see the world through the eyes of another person, and neither can I feel a pain that someone else experiences. When someone says that he has a toothache, I understand his language because I have also felt pain, perhaps a toothache. I *empathize* with the pains of others—literally, I 'feel with them', which is what etymologically 'empathize' means. Still, I am an outsider in their worlds. Neither how they see colors, hear noises, dream their dreams, nor how they experience pain belongs to *my* world.

Nevertheless, a common language and the apparent similarity between my experiences and those of others let me establish a bridge between my consciousness and theirs and to assume that they, too, are other *I's* just like myself. Obviously, with respect to objects like tables and rocks, this assumption does not work, because in all probability they experience nothing. With animals, too, there is a problem empathizing with what they seem to experience or understanding their reality. How does a squirrel see things and what awareness does it have of the world? We really do not know. That animals experience things and feel pleasure and pain is a fact that few are willing to deny, and it is difficult to agree with philosophers such as Descartes and Spinoza, who argued that in the natural world there is no consciousness other than human consciousness. For them, animals were gadgets produced by nature or created by God, not far above the level of clocks, unable to think or feel and devoid of consciousness.

Yet, anyone who has been attached to a pet or who has observed animal behavior knows that this is not true. Still, it is also true that whatever consciousness there may be in animals, the gap that separates human consciousness from theirs is immense and that even the most advanced chimpanzee lags behind the least intelligent person in terms of reason and understanding. Think, for instance, how difficult it would be to explain to a dog the contents of this chapter. The dog would look at us as we read the pages, unable to have even the faintest idea of what we are saying. On our part, we may have some idea of what goes on in the dog's consciousness but only a vague idea based on certain observable similarities of behavior, not a clear understanding of it. Why? Because its consciousness functions on a different level from ours, and because of this, dogs, we assume, do not have the ability to understand language, that is, *concepts*. In this sense, Aristotle was correct when he argued that the gift of speech has been given only to human beings. This gift allows us not only to utter sounds—animals also do that—but to use words and form them into statements through which we express thoughts and ideas. Through these, we give expression to our human consciousness, and through them, too, we structure the reality in which we live. Language is not merely a tool for communication, but a means through which reality emerges from our experiences. Neither is language simply the verbal expression of thought but, again far more than that, the very structure of thought, for which reason in the absence of language, there can be no thought. There is a sense, then, in which we can say that in speaking we create reality. This realization is well expressed in a statement of Heidegger, when he wrote that "words and language are not wrappings in which things are packed for the commerce of those who write and speak. It is in words and language that things first come into being and are."

Language, however, is not a matter that pertains only to the individual, as if he were a solitary consciousness existing by itself. For this reason, there are no private languages. Inevitably, the ability to speak is an endowment that every person shares with others. As a social reality, language is the bridge that allows every consciousness to be linked with those of others. Whenever I speak or write, I affirm the reality of the social context to which I belong and the undeniable fact that other minds aside from mine exist. Hence, while solipsism may be irrefutable, it stands challenged as soon as I use language for any purpose. As I write the concluding chapter of this book, am I not assuming that others will read it and even understand it? Philosophy itself is a long series of conversations among many minds that have tried to make sense of the world, and the same can be said of practically all human activities. Neither politics nor science nor education nor entertainment nor any other of the ways in which people are related to one another would exist if language did not exist. Even religion exists in terms of language: we *read* the Bible, *sing* hymns of praise, *confess* our sins, *recite* prayers, *profess* and *affirm* our faith, and *talk* to God. In all this, what is it that we do other than to use language? In so doing, do we not affirm that others, God or human beings, exist side by side with us?

Accordingly, if it is through language that the mind manifests itself and that reality is created—"things first come into being and are," to use Heidegger's expression—reality turns out to be a *social* construction in which we all participate and to which we all contribute in different ways and from different points of view. Berkeley's statement *esse est percipi*, therefore, needs to be reinterpreted and extended. To be or to exist is to be perceived or thought, not by my mind alone, but by the community of minds that constitute humanity. As the ground on which reality grows, consciousness is not a private affair but a social presence, as was recognized by Socrates, who sought to understand the human self—the soul—by searching for it not only within himself but also in others, the analysis of language providing for him the means to advance in his quest.

It is absolutely true that, as Descartes insisted, one's own consciousness is the most fundamental fact that can be affirmed. I may initially entertain doubts about all sorts of things—about what my senses tell me about the world, about the existence of others, about the reality of God. Yet, the fact that I have such doubts is a sure indication that *I* am thinking or that *I* am aware. In this thinking or in this awareness I discover the absolute fact that *I* exist as a consciousness—a *res cogitans* or 'thinking thing', in Descartes' language. I may even be uncertain whether my body is real, but I cannot doubt that *I* exist as the ground that makes that uncertainty possible. *This* fact cannot be doubted, which is expressed in that memorable phrase *cogito ergo sum*—'I think, therefore I am'. Still, the fact that I can *express* myself in language points to the reality of the social context in which I exist, and this context is one in which other 'thinking things' also exist. Hence, consciousness (mind, the ego, the soul, *I myself*, or however else we could express it) does not exist exclusively in me but is a reality that transcends my individuality. Accordingly, Descartes' *cogito ergo sum* ('I think, therefore I am') should be rephrased as *cogito ergo sumus*, that is, 'I think, therefore *we* are'. My awareness of myself as a conscious being reveals the presence of others, and this must be so if language is both the manifestation of consciousness and the matrix from which reality emerges. From this perspective of metaphysical subjectivism, reality does not exist independently of consciousness but is created by it, not only by my consciousness but by the consciousness that is present in every human being.

We can now return to Plato's allegory of the cave. What does it tell us about reality and about the nature of knowledge? It tells us that reality and knowledge are complex ideas that must be understood in terms of a multiplicity of levels. It also tells us that most people are unconcerned about the meaning of reality and that, like the prisoners of the cave, they assume that what they see and hear is real and that there is nothing more to say or think about the matter. The adventure of philosophy does not engage their imagination nor does it inspire them. To express it in Diogenes' language, few are those who even dream of becoming philosophers, for *that* would certainly distract them from their consuming activity of keeping track of passing shadows. For them, philosophy is a useless distraction, something with which nothing can be done.

The question is, however, not so much what we can do with philosophy, but what philosophy can do with us. It certainly did a great deal with the liberated prisoner. It awakened his mind—a mysterious occurrence that may not be explainable—and it impelled him first to question his experiences and those of others and then to search for a higher ground of understanding. Unsatisfied with what he had learned from childhood and with the normalcy of the common human world, he parted company with the 'reality' of most people. He liberated himself and moved away from it and let his mind wander in other regions where, he thought, true reality resides. He recognized the relative value of those things to which people attach so much importance and over which they struggle among themselves, like children fighting over plastic toys. He realized that neither time nor space are facts of the world but modes of knowledge through which, as Kant insisted, we structure our sense perceptions and introduce order into our experiences. This realization led him to seek a clearer light in which a more substantial reality can be found. This is the ascent out of the cave, steep and rugged and filled with difficulties, especially since it guided him progressively away from the 'reality' that floats indistinctly in the consciousness of most people. Above all, the liberated prisoner became aware that neither is sense perception a reliable source of information nor is the world revealed by the senses as real as we assume. The so-called objective reality of the ordinary world in which we live turns out to be an illusion of the senses, and the language in which we describe it is a collection of subjective opinions of little value, based on unstable impressions about unstable things.

The liberated prisoner understood at last that the world of illusion and opinion—the cave with its shadows—is a game in which we deceive ourselves with the mistaken thought that it is real and in which we are deceived by the games invented by others—those who move the objects that produce the shadows. In politics, for instance, they play the game of dividing the world into nations and having people kill one another over slogans and creeds that no one understands. In the world of science, the game is called 'Let us conquer nature', and the scientists —those prisoners who remember the greatest number of shadows and who predict their sequences—speak as if they had finally pinned down the ultimate truth. In education, the game has to do with forcing the youth to memorize bits of information, promising those who succeed a comfortable place in society. In religion, the game is played by using mysterious phrases and by practicing rituals and reciting prayers designed to dull the mind. And there are other kinds of games, all of which yield only this benefit, namely, allowing people to pass the time between birth and death without losing altogether their socially created sanity. From these games, however, the liberated prisoner is free. He has grown up and has broken the chains that had immobilized him for a long time. Understandably, however, he has become a nuisance among his fellow prisoners, who cannot wait for the moment when he parts company with them. And so, he leaves them, *compelled*, as Plato says, by a yearning to experience a different world.

In Plato's metaphysics, the world discovered by the liberated prisoner is vastly different from the world of the cave. Whereas the latter is only an illusion produced by sense perception, the former is a reality revealed by reason. There, in a dimension where neither time nor space nor change exists, where nothing comes into being or passes away, Being reveals itself to the mind as absolute reality. There, reason recognizes the Ideal Forms of which things in the physical world are imperfect copies, and crowning that real world is the Idea of the Good, the highest and most perfect reality that, like Parmenides' Being and Saint Anselm's God —'that anything greater than which cannot be conceived'—truly exists, investing all things with meaning and structure. But only a mind that has transcended sense perception can experience its presence, which explains why the liberated prisoner has at first so much difficulty accustoming his 'eyes'—the eye of the soul, to use Socrates' phrase—to 'see' the world outside the cave. Throughout his life, he, like most people, has only used his physical eyes and is only accustomed to experiencing physical things. It also explains why the inhabitants of the cave are unable to understand his language as he returns to tell them about his discovery. *Their* language, unlike *his*, is strictly based on sense experience and refers only to physical things. Thus, what *he* has 'seen' outside cannot be readily translated into *their* language, except perhaps through symbols and metaphors that can only point in a certain direction without disclosing a precise set of meanings. *They* hear *his* words without really understanding them. Perhaps, there is truly nothing that can be *said* about it. There is a statement in one of Plato's letters that supports this unsettling prospect. He tells us that philosophy, by which he means the experience of the world outside the cave, cannot be put into words but can only be directly experienced by the mind. We may talk about it in terms of analogies and through parables but cannot disclose its meaning in speech. We must leave the cave in order to understand what the outside world is.

There is an anecdote about Diogenes that can illustrate the difficulty of clarifying the reality that, according to Plato, lies beyond the physical world. Once, when Plato was talking about that reality, using terms such as 'the Ideal Form of a table' and 'the Ideal Form of a cup', Diogenes said to him, "Plato, tables and cups I see, but your ideal table and your ideal cup I cannot see." To which Plato retorted, "That is, Diogenes, because you only have eyes to see physical tables and cups, but lack intellectual eyesight to see what lies beyond physical things." At that point, Diogenes walked away, saying, "Plato's philosophy is a waste of time." This anecdote gives us a hint about *the* problem found in the human quest for reality. We should keep in mind that both Plato and Diogenes were philosophers, and both very clever men endowed with great clarity of mind. Thus, what we witness here is not the opposition between philosophical thought and unsophisticated chatter about the world. It is not that Plato was intelligent and Diogenes was not or the other way around. The problem is that in Plato and in Diogenes we come upon fundamentally different points of view that cannot be reconciled, almost as if they used mutually untranslatable languages. Diogenes did not understand or could not understand Plato's language, but neither was Plato able to see the world from Diogenes' point of view.

In another anecdote, we learn that once, when a disciple of Parmenides was intent on proving the impossibility of motion, Diogenes, *without saying a word*, got up and began to walk around him. All the arguments against motion, Diogenes must have thought, collapse under the weight of a simple observable act such as walking. The phrase 'without saying a word' is significant, because it points to the fact that sometimes philosophical disagreements are so profound that language is not sufficient to establish a common ground. We have all come upon situations in which we sense that our ideas are so different from those of others that we conclude that nothing can be said either to find an area of agreement or reach an understanding. In the human quest for clarity concerning reality, such situations are common. The conviction with which the materialist affirms that matter is the only real thing stands in sharp opposition to that of those for whom only consciousness exists, and building a bridge between them is seldom a successful undertaking. Sometimes even language fails to function as a meaningful common denominator when opposing views about reality face each other.

Still, philosophy itself has proved to be precisely the effort needed to examine experience and the world from a rational point of view and to find areas of agreement about the meaning of reality. As such, it has been a long adventure in the realm of ideas in which we can all participate and add our own contribution, no matter how small it may be. Understood as a search for meaning, which is how Pythagoras defined it, philosophy can help us make some sense of our human experience. Through it, what we sense, what we think, and even what we feel gain in structure and significance. It leads different people in the most varied directions, for, as we have seen, Plato's allegory of the cave has different meanings. For some, it may be an accurate representation of the human condition, and sense experience turns out to be only an illusion. For others, the world beyond the cave is an illusion created by those who have lost touch with the real world of physical existence. Still for others, like the skeptics, the cave has no exit and we are condemned to live our lives witnessing a procession of shadows about which there is nothing to say. The solipsist sits all by himself, convinced that the entire thing is only his own dream.

We can now recall once more Socrates' final words to the jury. The prospect of death does not disturb him, he says, because if there is another world, he expects to do there what he has done while in this world, that is, 'doing' philosophy, asking questions, exploring possibilities, seeking to unravel the mystery of things, making sense of experience. The idea of heaven as a beatific place where the soul contemplates passively and for all eternity the greatness of God, singing unending hymns of praise, and having discovered once and for all the ultimate truth—this idea does not appeal to him. In fact, had he heard about it, it would have been for him the promise of an eternal state of abysmal boredom. For philosophy with him, and surely with many others, was and is an adventure, an ongoing controversy about what is real, about what the ultimate constituents of the world are, about the nature of the human self, about the basis of moral values, about the existence of God, and about every thought and idea that may be present in the mind. As we reflect on the various themes explored in this and the preceding chapters of this book, we realize how complex the problem of philosophy is and yet how intellectually invigorating it is to be able to share in the adventure of wrestling with that complexity.

# Glossary of Names

**Anaxagoras** — Presocratic philosopher (fifth century B.C.). He was the first major philosopher known to have taught in Athens. His view of the world is pluralistic, for, according to him, the basic elements of nature, which he called 'seeds', are infinite in number. He thought of the universe as infinite in extent and as containing innumerable suns and earths. The processes of the universe, he believed, are guided by a cosmic force that he called *nous* (Mind).

**Anaximander** — Presocratic philosopher (sixth century B.C.). He was an associate of Thales. He is credited with the first book on philosophy. Important ideas are attributed to him, including the monistic view that the *arche* of the world is an element that he called the Infinite or the Indefinite. He conceived of the universe as infinite and eternal.

**Anaximenes** — Presocratic philosopher (sixth century B.C.). He was an associate of Anaximander and, like him, Milesian by birth. He identified the basic element or *arche* of the world with air.

**Andronicus of Rhodes** — Greek philosopher (first century B.C.). He is credited with the first edition of Aristotle's works. The word 'metaphysics' is derived from a title that he gave to one of these works.

**Anselm of Canterbury (Saint)** — Medieval philosopher and theologian (1033-1109). He is important for his views on the relationship between faith and reason. Faith, he argued, must precede reason in any attempt to deal with the nature of God. His ontological argument for the existence of God insists that the definition of God entails the fact of his existence.

**Aristophanes** — Greek playwright (c. 450-385 B.C.). Eleven of his comedies are extant. He used the comic stage as a means to voice his political and social concerns and to criticize the decadence that he discerned among the

Athenians. In the *Clouds*, he ridiculed Socrates, whom he viewed as a dangerous influence.

**Aristotle** — Greek philosopher (384-322 B.C.). In his younger years, he was a student of Plato in the Academy. He wrote voluminously on practically all areas of human and scientific concern. To him we owe the earliest classification of the sciences and innumerable insights about the universe and about human existence. Although deeply influenced by Plato, Aristotle eventually developed his own philosophical approach and came to his own conclusions. His approach is empirical: knowledge begins with sense experience, and the information gathered by the senses, when refined and extended through reason, furnishes us with accurate knowledge about the world. He maintained that reality is independent of the mind and that matter and form are the constituents of everything that exists. For him, happiness is the purpose of human life.

**Augustine (Saint)** — Early medieval philosopher and theologian (354-430). An important contribution of Saint Augustine was his attempt to build a bridge between classical philosophy and the Christian faith. For him, faith and reason are twin avenues that lead to God, although the former is safer and more direct. He dealt with a great number of philosophical issues including the problem of free will and the basis of moral values. His views were decisive in the formation of Christianity.

**Averroes** — Medieval Arab philosopher (1126-1198). He is important for his extensive commentaries on Aristotle's works and for his influence on Saint Thomas Aquinas.

**Bacon, Francis** — English philosopher (1561-1626). He advocated an inductive or empirical method for discovering the truth. This method has been the foundation on which science has been based since his time.

**Benedict, Ruth** — American anthropologist (1887-1948). Her foremost idea is the realization that "the concept of the normal is properly a variant of the concept of the good" and that the good is what society approves. Cultural relativism and ethical relativism are, therefore, intimately related.

**Bentham, Jeremy** — English philosopher (1748-1832). His contributions in ethics and political philosophy have had a significant influence on modern thought. He coined the word 'utilitarianism' as the name for his ethical theory. In this theory, utility is regarded as the only basis of moral values and is to be understood as that which promotes the greatest happiness and benefit for the greatest number of people. Ethics should be an empirical science in which utility (or happiness) can be measured by reference to a pleasure calculus.

**Berkeley, George** — Irish-English philosopher (1685-1753). The principal idea associated with him is his insistence on the primacy of consciousness as the determining factor for the structuring of reality. He rejected the reality of a material world that exists independently of the mind. Matter itself is a complex of experienced qualities that cannot exist apart from experience. The statement *esse est percipi* (to be is to be perceived) expresses well the essence of Berkeley's thought.

**Buddha** — Indian religious leader (sixth century B.C.). Gautama Buddha, as he is known, is the source of Buddhism, one of the principal teachings of which is the abandonment of material possessions and pleasures and the commitment to a life of simplicity and abnegation devoted to the alleviation of human suffering. The ultimate goal in Buddhism is the attainment of *nirvana*, a state in which desires and ambitions are extinguished.

**Clement of Alexandria** — Christian apologist (second century A.D.). He maintained that knowledge about God is impossible and that, while we must affirm his existence, we know nothing about his nature.

**Confucius** — Chinese philosopher (557-479 B.C.). More than a systematic and theoretical endeavor to understand the world, Confucius' philosophy is a collection of rules of conduct designed to help people live peaceful and virtuous lives. Its emphasis is, therefore, practical and ethical.

**Critias** — Sophist and Athenian politician (fifth century B.C.). From a fragment of his dialogue *Sisyphus*, we learn that he viewed the belief in the gods as a social mechanism imposed by the ruling classes on the masses for the purpose of controlling them through fear.

**Democritus** — Presocratic philosopher (c. 460-360 B.C.). Although he was one of the most prolific authors of antiquity, only fragments of his works have survived. His most important contribution is related to his view of the universe as an infinite collection of atoms (*atoma*)—small, indivisible, and eternal particles of matter. Things come into being and pass out of existence as a result of random combinations of atoms. The human soul (consciousness) is explainable in terms of atoms and their movements. His philosophy is an example of pluralism and materialism.

**Descartes, René** — French philosopher (1596-1650). Various scientific accomplishments are associated with him, especially in mathematics and cosmology. In philosophy, his methodic doubt is of great significance. He undertook the task of establishing knowledge on a firm and rational foundation. He argued that initially all ideas are doubtful, except the fact of one's own consciousness. "I think, therefore I am" is the basis of Cartesianism. On this basis he constructed a dualistic system, in which existence is viewed as composed of two kinds of things: extended things (physical reality) and thinking things (God and the human soul).

**Diogenes of Sinope** — Greek philosopher (c. 410-321 B.C.). His mode of life earned for him the title of 'the Dog'. The Greek for 'dog-like' is *kynikos*, from which words such as 'cynical' and 'cynicism' are derived. As the stereotype of a Cynic philosopher, Diogenes is associated with the rise of classical Cynicism. He despised social conventions and rejected the idea of nationality, calling himself "a citizen of the world." He practiced the most extreme kind of freedom of speech (*parrhesia*), and defined philosophy as the art of calling things by their right names. He advocated poverty, self-sufficiency, independence of judgment, and a commitment to a rationally structured life. For the extremes to which he carried his ideas he became known as "the Socrates-gone-mad."

**Empedocles** — Presocratic philosopher (490-430 B.C.). According to him, the elements of nature are earth, water, air, and fire, and from their combinations all things arise. These elements are uncreated and imperishable. Aside from the physical world, he taught, there is another dimension of existence to which the human soul belongs.

**Epictetus** — Greek philosopher (c. 60-110). He was an important Stoic philosopher. His philosophy is practical, its aim being to provide rational rules for virtuous living. He spoke of happiness as the goal of human life, but he understood happiness in the sense of *apatheia*, that is, the peace of mind that results from minimizing desires and maintaining impulses and emotions under rational control.

**Epicurus** — Greek philosopher (341-270 B.C.). He taught that happiness is and should be the only goal of human life. Happiness must be understood not in the sense of pleasure but as peace of mind. He assumed a negative stance toward religious beliefs and toward anything that distracts the mind with concerns other than those of the physical world.

**Freud, Sigmund** — Austrian psychologist and psychiatrist (1856-1940). Known mainly for the establishment of the psychoanalytic school, Freud wrote extensively on the origins of religion and on the human need to believe in God. He spoke of religious faith as an illusion, the roots of which are found in psychological maladjustments and societal influences.

**Gorgias of Leontini** — Sophist (c. 480-375 B.C.). He is associated with significant contributions to the study of language. He adhered to a radical sort of skepticism, maintaining (1) that nothing exists; (2) that even if anything existed, nothing could be known about it; and (3) that even if anything could be known, it could not be communicated through language.

**Gregory of Nyssa** — Father of the Church (c. 331-396). Rational understanding of the nature of God, he maintained, is impossible. Faith, therefore, is the only avenue that can lead us to knowledge about God.

**Heidegger, Martin** — German philosopher (1889-1976). His analysis of human existence has had considerable influence, especially among existentialist philosophers and writers. He explored in depth the role played by language in structuring reality.

**Heraclitus** — Presocratic philosopher (536-470 B.C.). He insisted on the unreliability of sense perception as a source of knowledge. Reason, understood in the sense of *logos*, is the only means to grasp the universal Reason (*logos*) or law that governs the world. Change is the universal condition that permeates all things. Heraclitus spoke of fire as the basic element of the universe.

**Herodotus** — Greek historian (fifth century B.C.). He is known as the father of history. His extensive account of the Persian Wars is one of the oldest historical books.

**Homer** — Greek poet (eighth century B.C.). He is traditionally believed to have composed several epic poems, the most important of which are the *Iliad* and the *Odyssey*.

**Hume, David** — Scottish philosopher (1711-1776). He is one of the most influential among modern philosophers. According to him, all knowledge is derived from sense perception, and all ideas, even the most abstract, are copies of simple impressions created by the comparison and combination of sensations. In ethics, he argued that moral values are explainable in terms of mental habits and social practices. Skepticism, in the sense of the denial of absolute knowledge, is a significant aspect of his philosophy.

**Jerome (Saint)** — Father of the Church (c. 340-420). In his early years he devoted himself to the study of Greek philosophy and literature and became an outstanding classical scholar as a translator and commentator. He made the first Latin translation of the Bible from the original languages. Later in his life, he turned toward fideism, arguing that faith alone can guide us to the knowledge of God.

**Kant, Immanuel** — German philosopher (1724-1804). His contributions in metaphysics, epistemology, cosmology, ethics, political thought, and aesthetics are many and most important. His metaphysics and epistemology are known as transcendental idealism, a view that maintains that reality is not independent of the mind but is structured by modes of knowledge (space and time) that belong to the mind. Space and time are the conditions that make knowledge possible. Although nothing beyond space and time can be *known*, Kant insisted on the need to accept what he called postulates of reason, specifically the existence of God, the freedom of the will, and the immortality of the human soul, which are affirmed on the basis of faith. Kant adopted ethical absolutism, a view that regards moral values as rational and absolute and that establishes morality on the basis of a universal law (the categorical imperative). Neither happiness nor any other consideration has any relevance in the formulation and the actualization of morality.

**Kierkegaard, Soren** — Danish philosopher (1813-1855). His works have been influential in the development of existentialism. His philosophical orientation was profoundly religious and was shaped by his adherence to extreme individualism. Intensely aware of the paradox and despair inherent in human existence, he sought to actualize in himself a deeply personal relationship with God.

**Locke, John** — English philosopher (1632-1714). His philosophy is one of the most consistent examples of empiricism. He denied the existence of innate or inborn ideas, and viewed the mind at birth as a *tabula rasa* on which, through sense experience, impressions are registered. According to him, all knowledge is the result of what we learn through the senses.

**Lucretius** — Roman philosopher and poet (98-54 B.C.). He was the author of a long poem entitled *On the Nature of Things*, in which he gave an exposition and a defense of Epicureanism. The materialism of Democritus is the basis of his conception of the world. He provided a clear statement of the argument from evil, which seeks to invalidate the belief in God.

**Maimonides** — Medieval Jewish philosopher (1135-1204). In his most important work, *Guide to the Perplexed*, he explored various issues, including the problem of the knowledge about God. He argued that the only way of speaking about God is the *via negativa*—we can say only what God is *not*, although we can attribute to him certain "attributes of action" such as his character as the creator of the universe.

**Marx, Karl** — German philosopher (1818-1883). His philosophical, social, and political ideas have exercised considerable influence in recent times. He adhered to materialism and to the conviction that human conditions are explainable in terms of socioeconomic circumstances. His economic and political views gave rise to the communist and socialist movements.

**Mill, John Stuart** — English philosopher (1806-1873). His philosophy is empirical, maintaining that sense perception is the only source of knowledge. He extended and refined Bentham's utilitarianism, introducing several ideas concerning pleasure. There are, he thought, various kinds of pleasures that can be classified vertically by reference to their desirability.

**Moore, George Edward** — English philosopher (1873-1958). In ethics, Moore's main contribution is related to his attempt to identify the basis of ethical values in terms of indefinable, yet very clear and precise, moral qualities that are accessible through direct intuitions. His ethics is, accordingly, known as intuitionism. He was particularly interested in showing the inadequacy of ethical naturalism as the basis of morality.

**Nietzsche, Friedrich** — German philosopher (1844-1900). Undoubtedly one of the most influential and best known among modern philosophers, he advanced revolutionary ideas concerning moral values that have been decisive in the development of existentialism. He opposed both the attempt to base moral values on religious convictions and the ethical nihilism that he saw permeating the European world of the late nineteenth century. He announced the death of God, by which he meant that moral values and aspirations must be based on the choices that human beings make for themselves.

**Paley, William** — English theologian (1743-1805). He maintained that the knowledge of God attainable through reason is a source of support for faith in God. He left a classical statement of the teleological argument, in which he compares the world to a watch and God to the watchmaker: just as the design of the watch points to the existence of the watchmaker, so does the design of the world show the reality of God.

**Parmenides** — Presocratic philosopher (fifth century B.C.). He had a profound influence on many subsequent thinkers, including Plato. Significant sections of his philosophical poem *On Truth* have been preserved. From them, we learn that he rejected sense experience as an instrument of knowledge and that he regarded the material or physical world as an illusion. True reality belongs only to a world that is accessible through reason.

**Phocion** — Athenian general and statesman (fourth century B.C.). He was one of the most respected men of ancient times for his honesty and moral principles. He was eventually executed for alleged high crimes against the State. He made it his practice to stand always in opposition to the opinions of the majority, arguing that if many people approve of an action, that action deserves to be condemned.

**Plato** — Greek philosopher (427-347 B.C.). In his youth he was an associate of Socrates, from whom he inherited his commitment to philosophy. After Socrates' death in 399 B.C., Plato undertook a series of travels and devoted himself to the study of mathematics. He returned to Athens around the year 394 B.C., where he taught and wrote until his death. He left us more than twenty dialogues, in most of which he assigns the main part to Socrates. In his mature years, he developed a complex philosophical system in which metaphysical, epistemological, ethical, educational, and political issues are integrated. Among the most important ideas associated with Plato are metaphysical idealism and dualism. The former maintains that true reality is found in Ideal Forms that transcend the physical world and that are discoverable only through the use of reason. Few philosophers have had an influence as great as that of Plato.

**Pyrrho of Elis** — Greek philosopher (360-270 B.C.). He is possibly the best representative of skepticism. He rejected the possibility of knowledge beyond immediate sensations. Since there is nothing that can be known, the best thing is to say nothing about anything, and the only solution is to suspend judgment about all things in order to attain peace of mind.

**Pythagoras** — Greek philosopher (sixth century B.C.). Important mathematical and astronomical contributions are attributed to him, including the Pythagorean theorem and a geocentric view in which the earth is conceived of as a sphere at the center of the universe. According to him, reality is made up of two levels, namely, matter and soul. The universe is governed by mathematical relationships, and number is the basis of all things. He is associated with the coining of the word 'philosopher', which means 'someone who searches for (or is a lover of) wisdom'. Although no writings are attributable to him, we have enough information to have a reasonable idea about his life and ideas.

**Sartre, Jean Paul** — French philosopher (1905-1980). A prolific novelist, playwright, and philosopher, he is associated with existentialism, which he defined as the conviction that human nature is created through choices and actions and that the only source of moral values is to be found in human existence. Existence, he contended, precedes essence, which means that there is no such a thing as a determined human nature or essence and that human beings are what they choose to be.

**Schopenhauer, Arthur** — German philosopher (1788-1860). His philosophy is possibly the best example of pessimism in its most extreme form. He regarded the world as bankrupt in all respects and human life as some sort of a mistake. In his metaphysics, the basis of all things is conceived of as a universal force that he called the Will, and all things as manifestations of this force. Blind, unguided, and voracious, the Will appears in all things and is responsible for the state of unhappiness in which most people live. The solution to the problem of human existence is to reject the Will by abandoning all desires and ambitions, especially the sexual urge, and by turning away from the Will and its manifestations.

**Socrates** — Greek philosopher (469-399 B.C.). Born in Athens, Socrates devoted his life to the pursuit of philosophy by questioning people about moral issues. His method of questioning, the elenchus, consisted in examining the language of his interlocutors—their definitions, assumptions, and conclusions. Although declared the wisest man in the world by the

Delphic oracle, he claimed that his only wisdom consisted in the recognition of his own ignorance. He insisted that self-knowledge is the goal of philosophy and that this knowledge is the necessary and sufficient condition for a virtuous and happy life. He was accused of corrupting the minds of the youth and of denying the existence of the gods. Found guilty by a jury, he was executed. Although no writings can be attributed to him, information about him is plentiful. Aristophanes, Xenophon, Plato, and others among his contemporaries wrote about him, and their reports, although not always consistent, serve as the basis on which we can reconstruct his life and philosophy.

**Spinoza, Benedict** — Jewish philosopher (1632-1677). He assumed a rationalistic stance toward religious beliefs and criticized the anthropomorphism that, in his view, plague Judaism and Christianity. His conception of God has been characterized as pantheistic: God and the world (or nature) are one.

**Tertullian** — Christian apologist (165-220). Tertullian's famous statement *"Credo quia absurdum est"* (I believe because it is absurd) sums up his extreme fideism. He regarded faith as the only avenue that can take us to God and reason as a distraction that can lead us astray.

**Thales of Miletus** — Presocratic philosopher (sixth century B.C.). He is traditionally regarded as the father of philosophy, because reliable information about earlier philosophers is unavailable. Nothing in writing can be ascribed to him. Important scientific accomplishments are associated with him, including the first cosmological model of the universe and the prediction of a solar eclipse in 585 B.C. He explained the world in terms of one universal element, or *arche*, which he identified with water.

**Theodorus of Cyrene** — Greek philosopher (fourth century B.C.). His radical atheism earned for him the name of 'the Atheist'. According to him, the belief in God or gods stems from ignorance and poor judgment.

**Thomas Aquinas (Saint)** — Medieval philosopher and theologian (1225-1274). One of the most influential thinkers of medieval times, Saint Thomas created a complex philosophical system in which he integrated Christian theology and Greek philosophy (especially Aristotle's ideas). His views became the intellectual basis of Christian theology. For him, faith and reason are parallel ways that lead to the knowledge of God.

**Thoreau, Henry David** — American philosopher (1817-1862). As evidenced in his writings and the style of his life, he adhered to firm moral principles and to the ideal of self-sufficiency. His individualism was manifested in his opposition to the laws and in his conviction that legality and morality are not always the same.

**Thrasymachus of Chalcedon** — Sophist (fifth century B.C.). Most of our information about him comes from Plato's dialogues where he is depicted as a Sophist who rejected all moral values except those based on power. His ethics can be summed up in the phrase "Might makes right." Ethical nihilism can be associated with him.

**Voltaire** — French philosopher (1694-1778). Born François Marie Arouet, Voltaire is one of the most important philosophical and literary figures of the eighteenth century. His writings address theological, philosophical, social, and political issues, among others. He regarded God as real but as detached from the world, an idea known as deism.

**Wittgenstein, Ludwig** — Austrian philosopher (1889-1951). One of the most influential philosophers in the twentieth century, he approached philosophy by means of the analysis of language, initially attempting to develop a formal structure in which language, especially the language used in scientific discourse, could be tested for meaningfulness, and subsequently moving into the domain of ordinary language. He argued consistently that before we can become engaged in exploring concepts such as reality and world, we must understand precisely the limits and parameters of the language in which our views are expressed.

**Xenophanes** — Presocratic philosopher (c. 570-480 B.C.). Two important ideas are associated with Xenophanes: (1) the belief that all living creatures have a natural origin and (2) the conviction that the gods of polytheism are only ways in which we speak of one and the same universal God. In Xenophanes' philosophy we come upon the earliest manifestation of monotheism among the Greeks.

**Xenophon** — Greek general and historian (430-354 B.C.). In his youth, he was an associate of Socrates. In his writings devoted to Socrates, he left valuable information about Socrates' life and ideas. These writings include the *Memorabilia*, which is a series of memoirs of Socrates, and the *Apology*, in which he gives an account of various themes related to Socrates' trial.

# Glossary of Philosophical Terms

**A posteriori** — A Latin phrase that denotes the knowledge that is derived from sense experience. Whatever is furnished by the senses (colors, shapes, smells, sounds, and other impressions) is a posteriori knowledge.

**A priori** — A Latin phrase used to designate the kind of knowledge that is *not* dependent on sense experience. Mathematical knowledge, for instance, is said to be a priori, because it is based on definitions and rational analysis.

**Agnosticism** — A view that denies that absolute knowledge is attainable. With respect to the existence of God, the agnostic, while not denying it, contends that conclusive evidence about it cannot be found. The word 'agnostic' is derived from two Greek words that mean 'no knowledge'.

**Anarchism** — The rejection of social and political authority. The anarchist rejects all political arrangements, including the State, and maintains that with respect to his own affairs he is the sole source of law.

**Ancient philosophy** — The first stage in the history of philosophy, beginning with Thales in the early sixth century B.C. and ending at the conclusion of classical times during the fifth and sixth centuries A.D. Most of the philosophers who belonged to this period were Greek or Roman.

**Animism** — A term that refers to the habit of investing inanimate things with qualities found in living things, especially with consciousness.

**Anthropomorphism** — The tendency of attributing to nonhuman beings or things human characteristics. The gods of polytheism, for instance, were believed to resemble human beings. Through anthropomorphic transformations, animals and inanimate objects behave as if they were human. The attribution of a masculine gender to God (God is male, a father, and so forth) may be interpreted as a vestige of anthropomorphism.

*Apatheia* — A Greek word that describes the conception of happiness advocated in Stoicism. Happiness, according to the Stoics, is found in a life in which emotions and feelings are kept under strict rational control.

*Apeiron* — A Greek term that is significant in the philosophy of Anaximander. It means 'unlimited', 'indefinite', or 'infinite', words that are associated with his description of the primordial element (*arche*) of the universe.

*Arche* — A Greek word that can be translated as 'beginning', 'origin', 'basis', or 'element'. Among the Presocratics, *arche* conveyed the idea of the basic element out of which things are made. In monism, as exemplified in Thales' philosophy, water was conceived of as the universal *arche*.

*Arete* — A Greek word generally translated as 'virtue'. The Greek word has a more specific meaning. It is used in the sense of 'strength' or 'excellence'.

**Argument from consensus** — The contention that the almost universal belief in God is a powerful argument for accepting his existence as an incontrovertible fact.

**Argument from design** — See **Teleological argument**.

**Argument from evil** — An argument that seeks to disprove the existence of God by pointing to the evil that in the form of pain and suffering permeates the world. If God is conceived of as omnipotent, omniscient, and benevolent, the reality of evil shows that such a God cannot exist.

**Asceticism** — From the Greek word for 'discipline' (*askesis*). A common element in asceticism is the conviction that pleasure is intrinsically bad and must be avoided.

**Atheism** — The denial of the existence of God or gods. The atheist affirms that there is no evidence that can lead us to affirm that God exists and that the concept of God transcends the limits of human knowledge.

*Atoma* — A Greek word that means 'indivisible' or 'unbreakable'. Democritus explained the universe in terms of exceedingly small *atoma*.

**Behaviorism** — A school of psychology that maintains that the traditional subject of psychology—the human mind—must be approached from an empirical point of view. In behaviorism, concepts such as mind and consciousness are abandoned and replaced with behavioral manifestations and responses that can be empirically studied.

**Categorical imperative** — In Kant's ethics, the moral law that is the only basis on which moral values can be established. It is a universal and absolute ethical commandment that has two formulations: (1) Act always as if your actions were to become a universal law (or rule) for all human beings, and (2) Treat all human beings (including yourself) as if they were ends in themselves, not means toward an end.

**Cosmological argument** — A line of reasoning, especially associated with Saint Thomas Aquinas, in which we argue that every event requires a sufficient cause that is responsible for its existence. An uncaused event is, therefore, an impossibility. The universe, conceived of as a chain of causes and events, must have had a first cause, and this first cause is what we call God. While this argument may not *prove* the existence of God, Saint Thomas proposed it as a way to render our belief in God reasonable.

**Cosmology** — The area of philosophy and science that deals with the nature and structure of the universe (*kosmos*).

**Cultural relativism** — An anthropological and sociological theory that recognizes the varieties of customs and practices among people and that maintains that moral values are the expression of customs and practices. In cultural relativism, 'good' and 'normal' are equivalent terms.

**Cynicism** — In its classical sense, Cynicism designates a philosophical movement that originated with Antisthenes (an associate of Socrates) and with Diogenes of Sinope in the fourth century B.C., and that remained in existence until the end of classical times. Its name is derived from the Greek word *kynikos*, which means 'dog-like'. The classical Cynics were known for their defiant attitude toward social conventions and norms, and for their commitment to a rational life in which needs and desires are minimized. Modern cynicism generally denotes an attitude of distrust toward ethical and social values and a rejection of the need to be socially involved. For an examination of classical Cynicism and its relationship to modern cynical attitudes, see L. E. Navia, *Classical Cynicism: A Critical Study*.

***De facto*** — A Latin phrase used to characterize statements about a factual condition. Assertions or statements of fact are said to be *de facto* and can be contrasted with *de jure* statements that convey the sense of the way things ought to be.

***De jure*** — A phrase (from the Latin word *ius*, which means 'right' or 'what ought to be') that distinguishes moral statements from factual statements. *De jure* statements are those in which we express ethical or moral judgments.

**Determinism** — The view that regards all events, including human actions, as determined or caused by antecedent conditions. Everything that happens is the result of necessary and sufficient causes. Consequently, neither randomness in the natural world nor freedom of the will in human life can be used as a means to explain events.

**Dualism** — The view that maintains that reality includes two levels of existence: a physical or material level and a spiritual level. A human being, for example, is composed of a physical body and a spiritual soul. In the philosophies of Plato and Descartes we come upon examples of metaphysical dualism.

**Elenchus** — The method of interrogation used by Socrates in his search for the definitions of moral terms. The purpose of the Socratic elenchus was to compel people to examine the meanings of the words in which they expressed their moral convictions. This examination, Socrates hoped, would lead to the recognition of their intellectual confusion, which, in its turn, would allow them to achieve a clear understanding of themselves.

**Empiricism** — The epistemological view that maintains that knowledge is based on sense perception. Observation is, therefore, the foundation of what we know, and ideas, regardless of how abstract they may be, are formed from the information provided by the senses. In empiricism, all knowledge is a posteriori. Locke and Hume are examples of empirical philosophers. Modern science has generally adopted an empirical stance in its efforts to understand the world.

**Epicureanism** — The school of philosophy established in Athens by Epicurus in the fourth century B.C. The fundamental belief of Epicureanism is that happiness is the goal of human life, happiness understood in the sense of tranquillity and peace of mind. The modern word 'epicure', while derived from the name of the founder of Epicureanism, does not reflect his idea of happiness. Whereas 'epicure' conveys the sense of someone who seeks pleasure, an Epicurean was someone who sought happiness through the use of reason.

***Episteme*** — A Greek word that can be translated as 'knowledge', 'science', or 'information'. *Episteme* in the sense of acquaintance or information is often contrasted with *sophia* or understanding.

**Epistemology** — The area of philosophy that deals with the problem of human knowledge. Three issues are at the core of epistemology: the nature of knowledge, the sources of knowledge, and the limits of knowledge.

***Esse est percipi*** — A Latin phrase that means 'to be is to be perceived' and that is used in the context of the metaphysical subjectivism of Berkeley. According to him, existence is entirely a function of perception and, ultimately, of consciousness. Nothing exists independently of consciousness.

**Ethical absolutism** — An ethical view in which moral values are said to be based on universal and absolute standards, as in the instance of Kant's ethics.

**Ethical egoism** — The attitude that justifies actions on the basis that they promote the advantage or benefit of the individual who undertakes them. The egoist, therefore, chooses only actions that promote his own welfare.

**Ethical emotivism** — The theory that interprets moral values as expressions of emotions or feelings. Ethical statements in which we use terms such as 'good' and 'bad', 'right' and wrong', express psychological states of mind or emotive preferences.

**Ethical hedonism** — See **Hedonism**.

**Ethical naturalism** — The ethical theory that defines moral terms such as 'good' and 'bad' in terms of characteristics or conditions that are said to be natural in human beings.

**Ethical nihilism** — The view or attitude in which moral values are regarded as basically meaningless. Ethical judgments cannot be based on anything that transcends the choices of the individual.

**Ethical rationalism** — The conviction that moral values must be grounded on strictly rational principles that are universal and unchanging.

**Ethical relativism** — The view that moral values are the expression of customs, practices, and traditions and that there is no other basis for morality. What is normal is, therefore, what is good. The ethical relativist derives moral values from what is accepted. What is accepted in a society is what should be acceptable in that society. There are no universal or absolute moral standards.

**Ethical subjectivism** — The conviction that moral values depend entirely on the choices and preferences of the individual.

**Ethics** — The area of philosophical inquiry that deals with morality. Ethics studies the basis and meanings of moral values. One of the most important issues raised in ethical discussions is the justification of ethical and moral statements.

*Ethos* — A Greek word that means 'custom' or 'habit'. Words such as 'ethics', 'ethical', and 'ethnic' are derivations from *ethos*. Etymologically, the terms 'customary' and 'ethical' are equivalent.

**Etymology** — The study of the origins of words. In etymology, we trace the linguistic roots of words back to earlier languages. In the case of the word 'etymology', for instance, we discover that it comes from two Greek words: *etymos*, which means 'true' or 'genuine', and *logos*, which means, among other things, 'explanation' or 'account'.

**Eudaemonism** — From the Greek word for happiness (*eudaimonia*). An ethical view that maintains that happiness, understood in the sense of well-being, is the ultimate goal of human life. Aristotle's ethics is an example of eudaemonism.

*Ex nihilo* — A Latin phrase that means 'out of nothing'. Creation *ex nihilo* is the process in which we assume that something comes into existence from nothing.

**Existentialism** — This term refers to a philosophical movement or, rather, an attitude that became prominent toward the middle of the twentieth century. It is difficult to come up with a definition of existentialism, because it embraces a great number of ideas and orientations. Possibly, the only common denominator is the exclusive preoccupation with human issues and the conviction that there is no such a thing as a determined human nature. Human nature is chosen by each person through his actions. Existence (what we choose and how we live) precedes (comes before) essence (what we are). Kierkegaard and Nietzsche are often regarded as forerunners of existentialism, and Sartre as its principal representative.

**Fideism** — From the Latin word for 'faith' (*fides*). A view that maintains that the belief in God is and should be based only on faith and that the premises on which religion is accepted should not be subjected to critical examination. Rational arguments, according to fideism, are inconsequential efforts either to support or to undermine religious convictions.

**Hedonism** — From the Greek word for pleasure (*hedone*). Hedonism has two general meanings: (1) psychological hedonism, a theory that explains all actions in terms of the natural human tendency to seek pleasure and avoid pain; and (2) ethical hedonism, a view that maintains that pleasure is what *ought* to be sought and pain is what *ought* to be avoided. Human behavior, according to psychological hedonism, is determined by pleasure and pain. According to ethical hedonism, pleasure and pain are the basis of moral values.

**Hylomorphism** — A term derived from the Greek words for 'matter' (*hyle*) and 'form' (*morphe*). Aristotle's metaphysics is generally interpreted as an example of hylomorphism because of its insistence that existence can be attributed only to things in which matter and form coalesce into a substance. From the point of view of hylomorphism, neither unformed matter (matter without a specific form), nor immaterial forms can be said to exist in a real sense.

**Hypothetical imperative** — An ethical statement in which we affirm that if a course of action is chosen, then certain conditions will follow from it. The presence of the *if-then* relationship between the two clauses of the statement is what renders it hypothetical. For instance, a statement such as "If I want to be happy, then I must obey God's commands" is a hypothetical imperative.

**Intellectual optimism** — This phrase refers to the belief that knowledge is the sufficient and necessary condition for moral goodness. According to Socrates, to know the good is equivalent to doing the good, and all evil is the result of ignorance.

**Intuitionism** — The ethical theory that maintains that moral qualities cannot be defined in terms of natural qualities or, in fact, in terms of anything else, because they are indefinable and simple. Moral qualities can be grasped directly only by means of an intuition that allows us to recognize what is good. Neither intentions nor consequences have any bearing on the import of what is good.

***Kosmos*** — A Greek word used initially as an adjective to denote beauty or order. With the Milesian Rationalists, however, it began to be used as a noun to designate the world at large or the universe, as in the word 'cosmos'.

**Logical positivism** — This term refers to a twentieth-century philosophical movement (known also as scientific empiricism) that insists that the primary function of philosophy is the analysis of language, specifically scientific language. It maintains that sense experience is the primary tool for the advancement of knowledge and that all statements must be judged by reference to the criterion of empirical verifiability: statements are meaningful only if it is possible to stipulate the conditions under which they can be verified in sense experience.

***Logos*** — A Greek word whose primary meaning is 'word', although it is used in the sense of speech, language, and explanation. It also conveys the idea of reason, both the human capacity to think and the order that permeates all natural processes. It can also be understood in the sense of natural law or regularity. In some traditions, God, as the structure of reality, is said to be the *logos* of the world.

**Materialism** — In ordinary speech, materialism is the tendency to attach excessive value to material things and possessions. In philosophy, materialism is the view that maintains that existence can be attributed only to material or physical things. Nothing aside from the physical world exists, except in function of something that is physical. Ideas and emotions, while not material, exist, but only as functions of the mind.

**Medieval philosophy** — A period in the history of philosophy that lasted about one thousand years, from the end of classical times to the beginning of the Renaissance. The dominant characteristic of medieval philosophy is the pervasiveness of religious and theological ideas. Medieval philosophers struggled with the issue of the relationship between faith and reason, assigning in most cases to the former the principal role as a vehicle in the task of understanding the world.

**Metaphysical objectivism** — The view that maintains that reality is independent of the mind and that things exist as they do, whether or not there is an observer or a consciousness that is aware of them.

**Metaphysical subjectivism** — See **Subjective idealism**.

**Metaphysics** — The area of philosophy that studies the meaning, nature, and structure of reality, existence, or Being. The word 'metaphysics' is derived from the title given to one of Aristotle's most important works, probably written after his *Physics.* In Greek, *meta ta physica* literally means 'after or beyond what is physical'.

**Milesian Rationalists** — This term refers to the three earliest philosophers, namely, Thales, Anaximander, and Anaximenes, who were born in Miletus, a Greek city on the southwestern coast of Asia Minor (present-day Turkey). Their commitment to explain the world in rational terms earned for them the designation of rationalists.

**Modern philosophy** — The period in the history of philosophy from the beginning of the Renaissance in the sixteenth century to the twentieth century.

**Monism** — The view that explains all things in terms of *one* element or principle. In the instance of the Milesian Rationalists, all things in the universe were conceived of as transformations of one material element or *arche.*

**Monotheism** — From two Greek words (*monos* and *theos*) that mean, respectively, 'only one' and 'god'. The belief in the existence of one universal God.

**Moral argument** — A theistic argument that seeks to demonstrate the existence of God as in indispensable foundation for moral values. In a version of this argument, we are told that if God does not exist, moral values are meaningless and human life has no purpose. Since, however, moral values must be meaningful and human life must have a purpose, God exists.

**Naturalistic fallacy** — Phrase coined by G. E. Moore to designate the mistake in reasoning committed by those who define moral words in terms of a natural quality. The fallacy consists in treating an indefinable word such as 'good' as if it were definable.

**Ontological argument** — An argument for the existence of God associated with Saint Anselm of Canterbury. It seeks to demonstrate that God exists by examining the essence or definition of God. By definition, God is a reality nothing greater than which can be conceived. A being nothing greater than which can be conceived is a perfect being. Perfection entails existence. Therefore God exists.

**Ostensive definition** — A definition in which we identify an object by giving an example of it or by pointing to it.

**Pantheism** — The belief that God and the world are one. The word 'pantheism' is derived from two Greek words, *pan* and *theos* ('all' and 'God'). Pantheism is associated with certain Oriental religions, as well as with the views of philosophers such as Spinoza.

*Parrhesia* — A Greek word generally translated as 'freedom of speech'. Its literal meaning, however, is 'saying it all', that is, the ability and willingness to use language to speak the truth under all circumstances.

*Petitio principii* — A Latin phrase that conveys the sense of 'begging the question'. In logic, *petitio principii* is a fallacy in which the conclusion of an argument is tacitly assumed to be true from the outset.

*Philos* — A Greek word that conveys the sense of 'friend', 'love', 'yearning', or 'desire'. Often understood in the sense of 'friend' or 'lover', *philos* was used by Pythagoras when he described himself as a philosopher, that is, a lover of wisdom.

*Physis* — A Greek word generally translated as 'nature'. Its meaning in Greek is more precise. It denotes the idea of process, change, or cyclical transformation. What is *physical* is what undergoes regular and predictable changes.

**Pleasure calculus** — A method proposed by Bentham to measure pleasures in terms of availability, intensity, duration, and other characteristics. This method, according to him, would furnish us with a precise idea concerning the degree of utility in human actions.

**Pluralism** — In the context of Presocratic philosophy, pluralism is the view that all things are composed of several elements or substances. According to Empedocles, these elements are earth, water, air, and fire.

**Polytheism** — From two Greek words (*polys* and *theos*) that mean, respectively, 'many' and 'God'. In polytheism, accordingly, a belief in the existence of a plurality of gods is accepted, as exemplified in the religious beliefs of the Greeks and the Romans.

**Pragmatism** — A philosophical movement originally defined and developed by Charles S. Peirce (1839-1914), and refined by William James (1842-1910) and John Dewey (1859-1952). The basic idea of pragmatism is well expressed in this statement of Peirce: "In order to ascertain the meaning of an intellectual conception one should consider what practical consequences might conceivably result by necessity from the truth of that conception." In pragmatism, therefore, the meaning, truth, and value of any idea can be found only in its practical consequences.

**Predestination** — The theological view that maintains that the omniscience of God makes it impossible for human beings to make free choices. Their lives and destinies are, accordingly, present in the mind of God from all eternity. The course of every human life, as well as the salvation or damnation of each person, are predetermined and unalterable.

**Presocratic philosophy** — The first period in ancient philosophy. It began in the early sixth century B.C. with the Milesian Rationalists and ended with the presence of the Sophists and Democritus during Socrates' time (late fifth century B.C.). Presocratic philosophy (literally, 'philosophy before Socrates') was initially launched as a series of theories about the universe and the nature of matter, and its orientation was objective, that is, directed at the world at large. In its final stages, especially with the Sophists, it reoriented itself toward human issues, specifically ethics and the study of language.

**Primary sources** — The testimonies about a historical person written by authors who were his contemporaries. In this sense, for instance, Plato's dialogues are primary sources for our information about Socrates.

*Psyche* — A Greek word that can be translated as 'soul', 'mind', 'consciousness', or 'self'. The notion of *psyche* is particularly significant in dualism, in which it often designates a spiritual level of existence that is beyond the physical world.

**Psychological hedonism** — See **Hedonism**.

*Res cogitans* — Literally 'a thinking thing'. A Latin phrase used by Descartes to refer to consciousness or the soul and contrasted with *res extensa*, which stands for physical things.

**Scientific empiricism** — See **Logical positivism**.

**Scientism** — A term that refers to the claim that science is the only avenue to advance knowledge. The empirical method of science is destined to dominate all aspects of human existence and is the only means through which reality can be known.

**Secondary sources** — The testimonies about a historical person written by authors not contemporary with him. In the case of information concerning Socrates, Aristotle's testimony about him is a secondary source.

**Skepticism** — The term 'skepticism' has various interrelated meanings. Its etymology takes us back to ancient Greek, where the verb *skeptomai* means 'to look for', 'to search', or 'to examine'. In philosophy, skepticism denotes the view in which absolute knowledge is regarded as inaccessible. In ordinary language, the word 'skeptic' is used in the context of someone who questions or is doubtful about the evidence presented by others.

**Socratic method** — The approach taken by Socrates in his quest for understanding. The Socratic method, also known as the elenchus, proceeds by questioning the key terms through which we express ideas and beliefs. Through this method, Socrates sought to force his interlocutors to examine their assumptions and to recognize their confusions and arrive at reasonable conclusions on their own.

**Socratic problem** — The problem of determining the biographical accuracy with which the primary sources (mainly, Aristophanes, Xenophon, and Plato) provide an account of Socrates' life and ideas.

**Solipsism** — A term derived from two Latin words, *solus* and *ipsus* (respectively, 'alone' and 'by itself'). In metaphysics, solipsism is understood as the view that reality exists only in the mind. There is, therefore, no external or physical world, and nothing, including other minds, exists. I (that is, my consciousness) am the only thing that I can be sure exists.

*Sophia* — A Greek word that means 'wisdom', or more precisely 'mastery' or 'understanding'. Together with *philos, sophia* furnishes us with the etymology of the word philosophy, 'the love of wisdom'. *Sophia,* in the sense of understanding, should be distinguished from *episteme,* in the sense of acquaintance or information.

**Sophist** — This word has two meanings. When capitalized, it refers to a group of philosophers of Socrates' time, known especially for their subjective orientation, their ethical relativism, their skepticism, and their ability to use language to support any argument (hence words such as 'sophistry' and 'sophism'). Gorgias and Thrasymachus can be cited as examples of Sophists. In its generic meaning, 'sophist' refers to a person of wisdom or *sophia,* from which we derive the word 'sophistication'.

**Stoicism** — A major school of philosophy in the classical world. The name of this school is derived from the word *Stoa* ('portico'), the name of an Athenian building where the Stoics would originally congregate. Stoicism emphasized the primacy of reason in human affairs and viewed the universe as guided by rational laws. The Stoics sought happiness in practicing *apatheia,* understood as the rational control of feelings and emotions.

**Subjective idealism** — A metaphysical view that claims that reality is basically a function of the mind. The world, from this point of view, is a creation of the mind. Independently of consciousness, therefore, nothing exists.

*Tabula rasa* — A Latin phrase that means 'blank slate'. In the epistemology of Locke, for instance, the mind is described as a *tabula rasa* before experience furnishes it with impressions, information, and knowledge.

**Tautology** — In its nontechnical sense, a tautology is a statement in which the definition of a term is already included in the meaning of the term. Tautologies (known also as analytical statements, identities, or equations) are true by definition. For instance, the statement "A triangle is a three-angle plane figure" is a tautology, because the relationship between 'triangle' and 'three-angle plane figure' can be expressed in terms of the identity sign ('=').

**Teleological argument** — A theistic argument that seeks to demonstrate the existence of God on the basis of the design of the universe and its individual components. A version of this argument contends that (1) it is clear that order and arrangement cannot be explained except by presupposing an intelligent organizer; (2) it is evident that order and arrangement are found throughout the world: (3) therefore, a universal intelligent organizer must exist; and (4) that organizer is what we call God.

*Telos* — A Greek word translated as 'purpose', 'goal', or 'destination'. In Aristotle's ethics, happiness is conceived of as the *telos* of human existence, and in the teleological argument for the existence of God, the order and design of the world reveal the *telos* for which it was created.

**Theism** — There are two beliefs associated with theism: (1) a belief in the existence of God, understood as eternal, omniscient, omnipotent, immanent, and benevolent, and (2) the conviction that there are valid rational arguments that can prove his existence or strengthen our belief in him.

**Theistic ethics** — A view that maintains that moral values are based on a divine authority (God) or in the teachings of a divinely inspired authority such as the Church. In theistic ethics, what is good is determined by the degree to which it reflects God's will.

*Theoria* — A Greek word that conveys the sense of 'vision' or 'view'. The word 'theory' is derived from it. Etymologically, a theory is an account or a comprehensive view of a number of facts and events through which we seek to explain their relationships. In Aristotle's language, theoretical knowledge is the knowledge that is sought for its own sake.

**Utilitarianism** — An empirical ethical theory named and developed by Jeremy Bentham, and extended and refined by J. S. Mill, that maintains that the basis of moral values is definable in terms of utility. The utilitarians understand by utility anything that promotes happiness, pleasure, benefit, and other similar conditions. An action is, therefore, good if and only if it brings about the greatest utility among the greatest number of people.

*Via negativa* — A theological view that maintains that the only possible way in which we can speak about God is by saying what he is *not*. God, therefore, cannot be described in terms of any attributes, because his essence transcends everything that is knowable through reason and through sense perception.

# Select Bibliography

Ackrill, J. L. "Aristotle on Eudaimonia." In *Essays on Aristotle's Ethics.* Edited by
   A. Rorty. Berkeley: University of California Press, 1980, pp. 15-34.
Adams, E. M. *Ethical Naturalism and the Modern World-View.* Westport, Conn.:
   Greenwood Press, 1973.
Anderson, R. "Socratic Reasoning in the Euthyphro." *The Review of Metaphysics*
   22 (1969), pp. 421-481.
Annas, J., and J. Barnes. *The Modes of Scepticism.* Cambridge: Cambridge Univer-
   sity Press, 1985.
Anselm of Canterbury. *Basic Writings.* La Salle, Ill.: Open Court, 1962.
————. *A New, Interpretive Translation of St. Anselm's Monologion and Pros-
   logion.* Translated by J. Hopkins. Minneapolis: Banning Press, 1986.
————. *Proslogium.* La Salle, Ill.: Open Court, 1974.
Aristotle. *The Complete Works of Aristotle.* 2 vols. Edited by J. Barnes. Princeton,
   N.J.: Princeton University Press, 1984.
Atwell, J. *Ends and Principles in Kant's Moral Thought.* The Hague: Martinus
   Nijhoff, 1986.
Baldwin, T. *G. E. Moore.* London: Routledge, 1990.
Barnes, H. *An Existentialist Ethics.* Chicago: University of Chicago Press, 1978.
Barnes, J. *The Ontological Argument.* London: Macmillan, 1972.
Barrett, W. *Irrational Man: A Study in Existential Philosophy.* New York: Double-
   day, 1962.
Benedict, R. *Patterns of Culture.* Boston: Houghton Mifflin, 1989.
Bentham, J. *An Introduction to the Principles of Morals and Legislation.* In *The
   Utilitarians.* Garden City, N.Y.: Doubleday Anchor, 1973.
————. *The Works of Jeremy Bentham.* St. Claire Shores, Mich.: Scholarly Press,
   1976.
Berger, F. R. *Happiness, Justice, and Freedom: The Moral and Political Philoso-*

phy of John Stuart Mill. Berkeley: University of California Press, 1984.

Bergmann, G. *The Metaphysics of Logical Positivism.* New York: Longmans, Green & Co., 1954.

Bernstein, J. *Nietzsche's Moral Philosophy.* Cranbury, N.J.: Fairleigh Dickinson University Press, 1987.

Black, M. "The Gap Between 'Is' and 'Should'." In *The Is-Ought Question.* Edited by W. D. Hudson. London: Macmillan, 1969, pp. 99-113.

Blackstone, W. T. *The Problem of Religious Knowledge.* Englewood Cliffs, N.J.: Prentice-Hall, 1963.

Bontempo, C. J. and S. J. Odell, editors. *The Owl of Minerva: Philosophers on Philosophy.* New York: McGraw-Hill Paperbacks, 1975.

Buckley, M. *At the Origins of Modern Atheism.* New Haven, Conn.: Yale University Press, 1987.

Burnet, J. *Greek Philosophy: Thales to Plato.* New York: St. Martin's Press, 1962.
————. *The Socratic Doctrine of the Soul.* London: H. Milford, 1916.

Burrill, D. R., editor. *The Cosmological Arguments.* New York: Doubleday, 1967.

Capaldi, N. *David Hume.* Boston: Twayne, 1975.

Capaldi, N., E. Kelly, and L. E. Navia. *An Invitation to Philosophy.* Buffalo: Prometheus Books, 1981.

Capaldi, N., E. Kelly, and L. E. Navia. *Journeys Through Philosophy: A Classical Introduction.* Buffalo: Prometheus Books, 1982.

Chalmers, W. R. "Parmenides and the Belief of Mortals." *Phronesis* 5 (1960), pp. 5-22.

Copleston, F. *History of Philosophy.* 7 vols. Garden City, N.Y.: Doubleday, 1961-1965.

Copp, D. "Moral Skepticism." *Philosophical Studies* 62 (1991), pp. 203-233.

Cornford, F. M. *Before and After Socrates.* Cambridge: Cambridge University Press, 1964.
————. *From Religion to Philosophy: A Study in the Origins of Western Speculation.* Sussex: Harvester Press, 1980.
————. *Principium Sapientiæ: The Origins of Greek Philosophical Thought.* New York: Harper Torchbooks, 1965.

Danto, A. C. *What Philosophy Is: A Guide to the Elements.* New York: Harper and Row, 1968.

Dawkins, R. *The Blind Watchmaker.* London: Longman, 1986.

Dover, K. J. "Socrates in the *Clouds.*" In *The Philosophy of Socrates: A Collection of Critical Essays.* Edited by G. Vlastos. Notre Dame, Ind.: University of Notre Dame Press, 1980, pp. 50-77.

Fann, K. T. *Wittgenstein's Conception of Philosophy.* Oxford: Blackwell, 1969.

Flew, A. *God and Philosophy.* London: Hutchinson, 1966.

Freud, S. *The Future of an Illusion.* New York: W. W. Norton, 1975.

Gillespie, C. C. *The Edge of Objectivity: An Essay in the History of Scientific Ideas.* Princeton, N.J.: Princeton University Press, 1960.

Gorman, P. *Pythagoras: A Life.* Boston: Routledge, 1979.

Gulley, N. *The Philosophy of Socrates.* New York: St. Martin's Press, 1968.

Guthrie, W.K.C. *Socrates.* London: Cambridge University Press, 1977.

————. *The Sophists.* Cambridge: Cambridge University Press, 1971.

Hare, R. M. *The Language of Morals.* Oxford: The Clarendon Press, 1952.

Hartnack, J. *Wittgenstein and Modern Philosophy.* New York: Doubleday, 1965.

Hartner, W. "Eclipse Periods and Thales' Prediction of a Solar Eclipse." *Centaurus* 14 (1969), pp. 60-71.

Heidegger, M. *An Introduction to Metaphysics.* Translated by R. Manheim. New Haven, Conn.: Yale University Press, 1964.

Hick, J. *Evil and the God of Love.* New York: Harper and Row, 1978.

————. *The Existence of God.* New York: Collier Books, 1963.

————. *Faith and Knowledge.* Ithaca, N.Y.: Cornell University Press, 1957.

Hume, D. *Enquiries Concerning the Human Understanding and Concerning the Principles of Morals.* Oxford: The Clarendon Press, 1951.

————. *A Treatise of Human Nature.* Oxford: The Clarendon Press, 1973.

Kant, I. *Critique of Practical Reason and Other Writings in Moral Philosophy.* Translated by L. W. Beck. Chicago: University of Chicago Press, 1949.

————. *The Critique of Pure Reason.* Translated by N. K. Smith. London: Macmillan & Co., 1961.

Kelly, E., and L. E. Navia, editors. *The Fundamental Questions: A Selection of Readings in Philosophy.* Dubuque, Iowa: Kendall/Hunt Publishing Company, 1997.

Kenny, A. *Descartes.* New York: Random House, 1968.

————. *The Five Ways: St. Thomas Aquinas' Proofs of God's Existence.* London: Routledge, 1969.

Kierkegaard, S. *Selections from the Writings of Kierkegaard.* Garden City, N.Y.: Doubleday, 1960.

Kirk, G. S., and J. E. Raven. *The Presocratic Philosophers.* New York: Cambridge University Press, 1960.

Kraut, R. *Aristotle on the Human Good.* Princeton, N.J.: Princeton University Press, 1989.

————. *Socrates and the State.* Princeton, N.J.: Princeton University Press, 1984.

LeMahieu, D. L. *The Mind of William Paley: A Philosopher and His Age.* Lincoln, Nebr.: University of Nebraska Press, 1976.

Lloyd, G.E.R. *Early Greek Science: Thales to Aristotle.* New York: W. W. Norton, 1970.

Locke, J. *An Essay Concerning Human Understanding.* Oxford: The Clarendon Press, 1976.

Lucretius. *De rerum natura.* Translated by W.H.D. Rouse and revised by M. F. Smith. Cambridge, Mass.: Harvard University Press, 1975.

Madden, E. H., and P. H. Hare. *Evil and the Concept of God.* Springfield, Ill.: Charles C. Thomas, 1968.

Mascall, E. *Christian Theology and Natural Science.* London: Shoestring, 1956.

Matczack, S. A. "Fideism." In *New Catholic Encyclopedia.* 17 vols. New York: McGraw-Hill, 1981, Vol. 5, pp. 908-910.

Matson, W. I. *The Existence of God.* Ithaca, N.Y.: Cornell University Press, 1965.

Mehta, J. L. *The Philosophy of Martin Heidegger.* New York: Harper Torchbooks, 1971.

Mill, J. S. *Mill's Ethical Writings.* Edited by J. B. Schneewind. New York: Collier Books, 1965.

———. *Mill's Utilitarianism: Text and Criticism.* Edited by J. M. Smith, and E. Sosa. Belmont, Calif.: Wadsworth, 1969.

Moore, G. E. *The Philosophy of G. E. Moore.* Edited by P. A. Schilpp. Evanston, Ill.: Northwestern University Press, 1942.

Munitz, M. K. *The Mystery of Existence.* New York: New York University Press, 1974.

———. *Space, Time, and Creation: Philosophical Aspects of Scientific Cosmology.* New York: Collier Books, 1961.

———. *The Ways of Philosophy.* New York: Macmillan, 1979.

Murray, G. *Aristophanes: A Study.* Oxford: The Clarendon Press, 1965.

Navia, L. E. *Classical Cynicism: A Critical Study.* Westport, Conn.: Greenwood Press, 1996.

———. *Diogenes of Sinope: The Man in the Tub.* Westport, Conn.: Greenwood Press, 1998.

———. *The Philosophy of Cynicism: An Annotated Bibliography.* Westport, Conn.: Greenwood Press, 1995.

———. *The Presocratic Philosophers: An Annotated Bibliography.* New York: Garland Publishing, 1993.

———. *Pythagoras: An Annotated Bibliography.* New York: Garland Publishing, 1990.

———. *The Socratic Presence: A Study of the Sources.* New York: Garland Publishing, 1993.

———. *Socratic Testimonies.* Lanham, Md.: University Press of America, 1987.

Navia, L. E., and E. Kelly, editors. *Ethics and the Search for Values.* Buffalo: Prometheus Books, 1980.

Nielsen, K. *Ethics Without God.* Buffalo: Prometheus Books, 1989.

————. "Why Should I Be Moral?" In *Introductory Readings in Ethics*. Edited by W. K. Frankena, and J. T. Granrose. Englewood Cliffs, N.J.: Prentice Hall, 1974, pp. 473-492.

Nietzsche, F. *Basic Writings*. Translated by W. Kaufmann. New York: Modern Library, 1968.

Paley, William. *The Principles of Moral and Political Philosophy*. New York: Garland Publishing, 1978.

Paton, H. J. *The Categorical Imperative: A Study in Kant's Moral Philosophy*. Philadelphia: University of Pennsylvania Press, 1971.

Plantinga, A., editor. *Ontological Argument from St. Anselm to Contemporary Philosophers*. New York: Doubleday, 1965.

Plato. *The Collected Dialogues of Plato*. Edited by E. Hamilton. New York: Pantheon Books, 1961.

Quinn, P. L. *Divine Commands and Moral Requirements*. Oxford: The Clarendon Press, 1978.

Rosen, F. *Jeremy Bentham and Representative Democracy*. Oxford: The Clarendon Press, 1983.

Ross, W. D. *The Right and the Good*. Indianapolis, Ind.: Hackett, 1988.

Rowe, W. L. *The Cosmological Argument*. Princeton, N.J.: Princeton University Press, 1975.

Runes, D. D., editor. *Twentieth Century Philosophy*. New York: Philosophical Library, 1943.

Russell, B. *Why I Am Not a Christian*. London: National Secular Society, 1970.

Ryle, G. *The Concept of Mind*. Chicago: University of Chicago Press, 1984.

Sartre, J. P. *Existentialism and Humanism*. Translated by P. Mairet. London: Methuen, 1948

————. *The Writings of Jean-Paul Sartre*. 2 vols. Edited by M. Contat, and M. Rybalke. Evanston, Ill.: Northwestern University Press, 1974.

Schopenhauer, A. *Complete Essays of Schopenhauer*. Translated by T. B. Saunders. New York: Willey Book Company, 1942.

————. *The World as Will and Representation*. 2 vols. Translated by E.F.J. Payne. Indian Hills, Colo.: The Falcon's Wing Press, 1958.

Smart, J.J.C., and B. Williams. *Utilitarianism: For and Against*. Cambridge: Cambridge University Press, 1973.

Smith, G. H. *Atheism: The Case Against God*. Los Angeles, Calif.: Nash, 1974.

Smith, J. E. *Reason and God: Encounters of Philosophy with Religion*. New Haven, Conn.: Yale University Press, 1961.

Stevenson, C. L. *Ethics and Language*. New Haven, Conn.: Yale University Press, 1944.

Stone, I. F. *The Trial of Socrates*. New York: Doubleday, 1989.

Sullivan, R. *Immanuel Kant's Moral Theory.* Cambridge: Cambridge University Press, 1989.

Sylvester, R. P. *The Moral Philosophy of G. E. Moore.* Philadelphia, Pa.: Temple University Press, 1990.

Thomas Aquinas. *Basic Writings of Saint Thomas Aquinas.* New York: Random House, 1945.

———. *Philosophical Texts.* Fair Lawn, N.J.: Oxford University Press, 1960.

Thoreau, H. D. *On Civil Disobedience.* New York: W. W. Norton, 1966.

———. *Walden and Other Writings.* Edited by W. Howarth. New York: Random House, 1981.

Toulmin, S. *An Examination of the Place of Reason in Ethics.* Cambridge: Cambridge University Press, 1950.

Vlastos, G. "The Socratic Elenchus." In *Oxford Studies in Ancient Philosophy.* 4 vols. Edited by J. Annas. Oxford: The Clarendon Press, 1983, Vol. 1, pp. 27-59.

Voltaire. *Poem Upon the Lisbon Disaster.* Lincoln, Mass.: Penmaem Press, 1977.

———. *Selections.* Edited by P. Edwards. New York: Macmillan, 1989.

Watson, G. *Free Will.* Oxford: Oxford University Press, 1982.

Westermarck, E. *Ethical Relativity.* New York: Harcourt, 1932.

Wheelwright, P., editor. *The Presocratics.* New York: The Odyssey Press, 1966.

Williams, B. *Ethics and the Limits of Philosophy.* Cambridge, Mass.: Harvard University Press, 1985.

———. "Tertullian's Paradox." In *New Essays in Philosophical Theology.* Edited by A. Flew, and A. MacIntyre. New York: Macmillan, 1964, pp. 211ff.

Wittgenstein, L. *Philosophical Investigations.* Translated by G.E.M. Anscombe. Oxford: Blackwell, 1953.

———. *Tractatus Logico-Philosophicus.* Translated by D. F. Pears and B. F. McGuiness. London: Routledge, 1961.

Wong, D. B. *Moral Relativity.* Berkeley, Calif.: University of California Press, 1984.

# *Index*

## About the Author

LUIS E. NAVIA is Professor of Philosophy at New York Institute of Technology. He has written extensively in philosophy and is the author of fourteen books. His most recent books are *The Socratic Presence: A Study of the Sources* (1993), *The Philosophy of Cynicism: An Annotated Bibliography* (Greenwood Press, 1995), *Classical Cynicism: A Critical Study* (Greenwood Press, 1996), and *Diogenes of Sinope: The Man in the Tub* (Greenwood Press, 1998).

ISBN 0-313-30976-0

EAN

90000>

9 780313 309762

HARDCOVER BAR CODE